Praise for "Creating Startup Junkies ..."

"Creating Startup Junkies proves that entrepreneurship is everywhere - even in Arkansas! It's a must read playbook for anyone who wants to kindle innovation and entrepreneurship in their community."

- Steve Blank, Father of Modern Entrepreneurship

"Some places, like Arkansas and other "flyover states" are creating thriving entrepreneurial ecosystems. With specific examples and tips for often overlooked geographies, "Creating Startup Junkies" will help any "unexpected place" become more competitive in the global marketplace. "Creating Startup Junkies" provides you with the knowledge, the anecdotes, the tools, and the framework to create your own tribe of Startup Junkies - a tribe who will change the DNA of your entrepreneurial ecosystem, and in the process, transform the economic vitality of your community. Now, go get to work!"

- Congressman French Hill

"Jeff Amerine and Jeff Standridge, through their combined knowledge, experience, creativity, and success, have launched hundreds of dreams and careers. Now they have written a book that shares many gems of their advice. The book will fire the imagination of educators, economic developers, government leaders, and start-up junkies who no doubt will help launch hundreds more projects and products in flyover states such as Arkansas. Jeff and Jeff are members of an elite band of entrepreneurs who have fueled Arkansas's reputation as a global leader in the development of technology that makes life better for everyone."

- Asa Hutchinson, Arkansas Governor

"The University of Central Arkansas is a proud partner with Startup Junkie through the Conductor enterprise. As a vibrant, comprehensive university, UCA offers a talented student body, an innovative faculty and staff, and a mission of external engagement that - via our partnership with Conductor - ensures that our university is bolstering the pillars of talent, culture, and community engagement to attract financial capital investments into our human capital and our region. The Conway area continues to punch far above its weight because of this innovative culture that is committed to growing and attracting talent."

- Houston Davis, Ph.D.,
President of the University of Central Arkansas

"Our economy in Arkansas is bolstered by the innovation of individual entrepreneurs. Walmart, JB Hunt, Tyson's, Murphy Oil and Dillard's were all startups by founders who overcame all the obstacles that face today's Startup Junkies. This book will help guide those who seek the same dreams of accomplishment, building success and creating jobs."

- Michael Preston, Secretary of the Arkansas
Department of Commerce

"These days, innovation is part of everybody's everyday job. The tech startups on both coasts of America are increasingly becoming bookends to a much broader, and frankly, more interesting range of new businesses coming out of the so-called "fly over states." Jeff Amerine and Jeff Standridge present a convincing case for flying IN to these little known places to listen, learn and frankly, to be amazed. This book is long overdue."

- Louis Palter, New York Times Best Selling Author
and President of The B.I.T. Group

"I've always been impressed by the extent to which Jeff Amerine has demonstrated that, regardless of geography, he can assemble the teams, resources, and plan necessary to create disruptive customer value. If North America wants to maintain a competitive position globally, we've got to double down on these best practices."

- The Hon. Colin Deacon, Senator of the Senate of Canada

"Amerine and Standridge know what they are talking about when it comes to building venture ecosystems because they are two entrepreneurs who have been immersed in building venture ecosystems in unexpected places. They have both been involved in mentoring new businesses and research shows very clearly that such mentoring increases the probability of success. When it comes to talking about building venture ecosystems, it is not enough to have just been an entrepreneur, you must also have experience in investing in early stage ventures as well as mentoring them. They both have all of these requirements so this book should be a high value add to anyone interested in venture ecosystem building. Hopefully, many will have an interest in seeing venture ecosystems being built because it is important to the future of the United States."

- Matt Waller, Ph.D., Dean of the Sam M. Walton College of Business at the University of Arkansas Fayetteville

"In Creating Startup Junkies, Jeff Armine and Jeff Standridge demystify how would-be founders and community stakeholders can give rise to a thriving entrepreneurial scene by playing to a region's strengths. For oft-overlooked areas of the country, like Arkansas, this book is a manual for growth. Our state has a legacy of cultivating some of the most successful companies on the planet. With the guidance of the Startup Junkie team, the foundation is being laid for the next JB Hunt, Tysons, or Walmart to take the world by storm. As a proud member of a fourth-generation family enterprise that was launched in my hometown of Hope, I can't wait to see these pages put into practice by tomorrow's entrepreneurs."

- Mack McLarty, Chairman of McLarty Associates and Former White House Chief of Staff

"I wish I had this book 33 years ago when starting our company. This is a great roadmap for entrepreneurs in Arkansas and everywhere. It's an invaluable resource for those starting companies from new or reinventing themselves for the future."

- Sam Alley, VCC Co-Founder and CEO

"The two Jeff's have long been important to the entrepreneurial development of Arkansas. As they identified in the Four Pillars of Ecosystem Building, they argue that talent is the most important element. They have that in spades and have written an important book for entrepreneurs, policy makers, investors, business leaders, educators, and students."

- Ed Bashaw, Dean and Jones Distinguished Professor at Emporia State University School of Business

"Arkansas serves as an example of innovation and entrepreneurial spirit in the heartland. Creating Startup Junkies provides a framework for similar states and communities to follow to foster a collaborative ecosystem where entrepreneurship can thrive. The book is a must-read for ecosystem builders taking a look at the assets and gaps in their community and creating a strategy for a sustainable ecosystem."

- Ellen Bateman, Director for U.S. Ecosystems for the Global Entrepreneurship Network

"Jeff Standridge and Jeff Amerine are strong leaders in building entrepreneurial ecosystems. In this book they share their experience and knowledge, saving entrepreneurs years of learning the hard way. Their work covers all aspects of the start-up process from idea generation to the successful launch of an enterprise. The discipline they show in guiding innovators is an advantage to those they have coached. Standridge and Amerine combine to form a powerful team and they are willing to share their ideas on succeeding in the world of entrepreneurship. Their goal with this book is to help people bring innovations to market and to make the lives of others better along the way."

- Barry Brady, Chief Operating Officer, Arkansas Children's Research Institute

"The team at Conductor/Startup Junkie have been transformational to our community as they've built out the entrepreneurial ecosystem here and in the 11 counties around us. Their pillars of Talent, Culture, Capital and Community Engagement should be followed by anyone wanting to better support existing businesses and the creation of new ventures. Creating Startup Junkies is a "must read" book for any mayor, economic developer, chamber executive or university president who wants to transform their community through the development of a sustainable entrepreneurial ecosystem."

- Bart Castleberry, Mayor of the City of Conway Arkansas

"Jeff Standridge has always been an innovator and visionary in his thinking and work, and "Creating Startup Junkies" is that spirit coming to life for all entrepreneurs and communities that want to build a thriving startup ecosystem. Supporting entrepreneurs in our towns and cities provides positive energy, growth and limitless economic development. Who wouldn't want to take this book and turn into action right away? We've seen them put this into action, and it works!"

- Jenna Compton, EVP and Chief People and Corporate Strategy Officer at Simmons Bank

"When you are on the journey we call entrepreneurship, it can be confusing and hard to find your way. Like any journey, what you need to be successful is a great guide. Amerine, Standridge, and the entire Startup Junkie/Conductor team are those guides. From being there whenever you need help, to always being one of your biggest cheerleaders, this team sweats and bleeds empowering entrepreneurs."

- Joe Ehrhardt, CEO and Founder of Teslar Software

"It wasn't long ago that it was possible to count the number of high-growth startups in Arkansas on one hand, but you would never know it today. By pairing culture-building events with world-class mentoring and consultation, through effective partnership and collaboration, and with seasoned visionaries at the helm, Startup Junkie has played a catalytic role in developing what is now a vibrant, diverse venture and investment scene across the state. If entrepreneurship is a team sport, Creating Startup Junkies is the ultimate playbook for entrepreneurship support organizations, policymakers, and community-builders across the Heartland and beyond."

- Sarah Goforth, Executive Director in the Office of Entrepreneurship and Innovation at the University of Arkansas Fayetteville

"Jeff Standridge, Jeff Amerine, and their team at Startup Junkie are committed to creating programs and processes that support entrepreneurial activity and help businesses compete, succeed, and grow. I have had the pleasure of working with their team on programs geared toward entrepreneurially minded students at the University of Central Arkansas and have also witnessed the positive impact their programs have had across Arkansas and the region. This book highlights the key components of their system – a system that has proven results."

- Michael Hargis Ph.D., Dean at the University of Central Arkansas College of Business

"Entrepreneurship is vital to the growth and vitality of our country, yet too much of our attention is focused on the coastal startups. Creating Startup Junkies demonstrates how any place can build sustainable venture ecosystems by focusing on the four pillars - Talent, Culture, Community, and Capital."

- Auren Hoffman, CEO of SafeGraph

"Launching a new venture is fraught with challenges and obstacles, even more so when attempting to do so in a community that lacks the kinds of institutional, cultural and economic support systems that can be so important to entrepreneurial start-ups. Many good resources have been developed for individual entrepreneurs, but not nearly as many for those interested in creating entrepreneurial eco-systems at the community level. 'Creating Startup Junkies' makes a significant contribution—including practical tools and actionable advice—to closing that gap."

- Jonathan Johnson, Chair of the Department of Strategy, Entrepreneurship, and Venture Innovation at the Sam M. Walton College of Business at the University of Arkansas Fayetteville

"Creating Startup Junkies is a must-read for anyone who wants to support a culture of entrepreneurship in their community. The new business growth rate in Fayetteville, Arkansas is a testament to Startup Junkie's expertise in building ecosystems where small businesses and entrepreneurs can thrive long-term."

- Lioneld Jordan, Mayor of the City of Fayetteville, Arkansas

"While it feels as though I've been studying and working in entrepreneurial ecosystems for decades, it really is still a nascent field. We know that the bottom-up, entrepreneur-led model works but we need more to change that dominant narrative. Examples like these – success stories like these coupled with smart lessons to take away – are essential. Ecosystems have become a hot topic and have attracted many good people (and, dare I say, a few hucksters). Whether I wear my ecosystem builder hat or my scholar hat, I'm impressed! These folks are the real deal."

- Norris Krueger, Ph.D., Ecosystem Builder, Scholar,
Educator, and Agent Provocateur

"Creating and nurturing an entrepreneurial ecosystem is important for any city or region. As our community looked at the best local option, it became clear that we needed a dedicated organization that could spend the time required and had the experience necessary to ensure the success of these endeavors. Through robust and diverse programming, consulting, and mentorship the Conductor has become our most important partner in assisting entrepreneurs and small businesses. They are a key piece of our local economic development strategy."

- Brad Lacy, CEO of the Conway Development Corporation
and Conway Area Chamber of Commerce

"My experiences with start up and early stage ventures had primarily been in the technology and service industries in a dozen international companies...until I ran into Start-up Junkies. After observing this team for a decade, I have been most impressed with their wide diversity of businesses and bandwidth of knowledge; their creative energy, focus, the discipline, the imagination, are truly remarkable. This team is easily the best I have seen...and I have seen quite a few....they expanded my own knowledge of new businesses and successful start up practices ten-fold."

- Ashton McCombs, President and CEO of Phigenics and Chair of Board for SLS Community

"In 2012, I became an entrepreneur. That decision was inspired in part by a rising entrepreneurial ecosystem in Northwest Arkansas led by the work of Startup Junkie and a number of community advocates. Since that time, our company benefited from and hopefully contributed to the talent, culture, capital, and community engagement of the region. I'm excited that Startup Junkie will be sharing that recipe with the rest of the flyover states and other unexpected places."

- Michael Paladino, Co-Founder of RevUnit

"Creating Startup Junkies: Building Sustainable Venture Ecosystems" is an excellent book for the aspiring entrepreneur, especially one who is coming from a university. The information in the book was gained from years of experience guiding faculty, staff, and students in the creation of high-tech start-ups. It is also an excellent reference for university leaders who want their institution to be an economic engine for their state and region."

- Jim Rankin, President of the South Dakota School of Mines and Technology

"Startup Junkie has cracked the code on a methodology for building a sustainable entrepreneurial ecosystem. They've coordinated the perfect balance of talent, capital, entrepreneurial culture, and community engagement. I saw it in action; with hard work, discipline and StartUp Junkie's tools; there is now proof that a region can make a transformation into an unexpected, thriving tech cluster."

- Daniel Sanker, Founder and President of CaseStack and Founder and Chairman of SupplyPike

"Creating a thriving startup ecosystem in unexpected places requires a careful coordination of resources, relentless education, and an unconquerable spirit. Jeff and the Startup Junkie team have been students and practitioners of this process for a long time. I'm glad they've finally been prevailed upon to put it all down in a book so the rest of us can benefit from their experience."

- Joe Saumweber, Investor, Advisor, and Co-Founder of RevUnit

"Here's the playbook for policymakers, community leaders and especially aspiring entrepreneurs. Anybody interested in accelerating the economic growth in their state or community, or growing a successful business, needs to study this game plan laid out by Amerine and Standridge. It's terrific and I strongly recommend you read it and act on it."

- Randy Zook, CEO of the Arkansas State Chamber of Commerce

CREATING STARTUP
JUNKIES

*Building Sustainable Venture Ecosystems
in Unexpected Places*

Jeff Amerine and
Jeff D. Standridge

High
Point
Publishers

Published by:
High Point Publishers
915 Oak St., Suite 1004
Conway, AR 72032

Library of Congress Cataloging-in-Publication Data
Amerine, Jeff and Standridge, Jeff D.

LCCN: 2020947235
ISBN: 978-0-9779340-9-6

Printed in the United States of America

Acknowledgments

This work simply would not be possible without the numerous entrepreneurs and investors with whom we have had the opportunity to work over the years. In addition, a hearty word of thanks goes out to the entire Startup Junkie Team, both in Northwest Arkansas (Startup Junkie) and in Central Arkansas (Conductor), to whom we owe a huge debt of gratitude.

Finally, we wish to express our appreciation and gratitude to the various Entrepreneurial Support Organizations across the State of Arkansas, and in other "unexpected places" around the world. Their work is having a huge impact on entrepreneurs and on communities, but it seldom gets the same level of recognition as those in the more well known locations.

Contents

Foreword

Over the past few years, the entrepreneurial movement in Arkansas has gained considerable momentum. Through a variety of public and private investments of time, talent and treasure, we have made significant progress in cultivating a thriving statewide innovation and entrepreneurial ecosystem.

As a former entrepreneur and industry leader in banking and technology, I understand the need to foster entrepreneurship for sustainable economic growth. While in Congress I served as the Co-Chair of the House Entrepreneurship Caucus and introduced the Enhancing Entrepreneurship for the 21st Century Act to investigate the decline of new entrepreneurial endeavors. One major asset Arkansas has had in addressing this "startup slump" is the work of the Startup Junkie and Conductor teams, which have helped lead the charge in entrepreneurial development and support in the state.

Jeff Amerine and Jeff Standridge have been leaders in that evolution. Throughout their careers they have changed Arkansas for the better. Jeff Amerine, Managing Director of Startup Junkie Consulting, began his career in entrepreneurial ecosystem development over a decade ago, pulling from his experience as a startup leader, a corporate executive, investor, university technology commercialization leader, and adjunct faculty member. Amerine and his network of colleagues, researchers, and business founders have made Northwest Arkansas a recognized startup hub of the South. He has grown his initial idea to support startup founders and innovators into a multi-national venture, helping communities across North America, Asia, and Europe to produce more fertile soil for their entrepreneurs to grow.

Dr. Jeff Standridge, Managing Director of the Conductor (a Startup Junkie brand), has used his leadership experience as a corporate innovator, change agent, intrapreneur, and tech executive to help entrepreneurs develop and define their products and services, helping thousands of founders bring their ideas to market. With special experience in healthcare, data analytics, and sales/marketing, Standridge is moving the needle in healthcare and big data.

Under the leadership of Amerine and Standridge, the Startup Junkie/Conductor teams have won multiple competitive contracts from the US Small Business Administration, the US Economic Development Agency, and the Arkansas Economic Development Commission. They work with the support of the Walton Family Foundation, the University of Central Arkansas, the University of Arkansas, regional Chambers of Commerce, and local municipalities. During my tenure in Congress, Amerine, Standridge, and their incredible team have raised millions of dollars in venture capital, advocated for entrepreneurial policy change at all levels of government, grown entrepreneurial education at multiple universities, and impacted the lives of over 20,000 entrepreneurs.

The Startup Junkie/Conductor teams owe much of their success to strengthening the Four Pillars of Ecosystem Development: Talent, Culture, Community Engagement, and Capital. The Startup Junkie method of ecosystem-building has proven to be successful regardless of industry or community served, helping Northwest Arkansas become a destination of choice for startups in the retail, software, and supply chain sectors as medical, data analytics, and manufacturing companies migrate toward central Arkansas. The Startup Junkie/Conductor teams are helping the full spectrum of entrepreneurs, from high tech/high growth startups to rural business owners on Main Street. They host the Fuel Accelerator for Artificial Intelligence companies, the 10x Accelerator for tech-enabled startups, the Health Sciences Entrepreneur Bootcamp, the Startup Crawl, 1 Million Cups, and the Startup Junkies Podcast, in addition to countless programs that unite communities and inspire, empower, and enable individuals to start and grow their own companies. Their Four Pillars of Talent, Culture, Community Engagement, and Capital work because they help to identify the existing entrepreneurial assets within a community and then provide a framework to strengthen and grow the unique ecosystem in that community.

Creating Startup Junkies is a book for anyone who wants to increase startup activity and strengthen their unique innovation and entrepreneurial ecosystem. The "Ecosystem Building Canvas" and "Strategic Initiative Planning Process," both of which you'll find in the book, are applicable to entrepreneurs and community champions who want to attract and retain startup talent, increase and nurture a collaborative culture that is not afraid to take risks, engage more effectively with community stakeholders, and infuse much needed capital into early stage ventures. Unexpected places like Arkansas and other "flyover states" can create thriving entrepreneurial ecosystems. With specific examples and tips for often overlooked geographies, *Creating Startup Junkies* will help any "unexpected place" become more competitive in the global marketplace. *Creating*

Startup Junkies provides you with the knowledge, anecdotes, tools, and framework to create your own band of Startup Junkies - a band that will change the DNA of your entrepreneurial ecosystem, and in the process, transform the economic vitality of your community. Now, go get to work!

- Representative French Hill, Arkansas
U.S. House of Representatives

PART 1:

Setting the Stage

CHAPTER 1:

Entrepreneurship in the United States

What is a Startup Junkie?

Entrepreneurs are the critical foundation of all thriving communities. Any amazing product, service, or movement that changed lives started with a wide-eyed entrepreneur at some point. Building something – anything, really – requires that spark from the one lonely soul that just could not tolerate the status quo another minute. The entrepreneur takes that first crucial step and says, "I can do this. I can solve this problem." That first determination begins a winding journey full of long hours, low (or no) wages, and no foreseeable finish line. For most, the motivation to begin this journey is not just the prospect of making money - entrepreneurs are motivated by notions of self determination, the freedom to create, and doing something meaningful.

The journey can be lonely, and the failure rate is high for entrepreneurs, particularly if their community does not have adequate resources or support measures available. An entrepreneur's community, which includes their physical place of being, personal and professional network, access to tools and information, and other other amenities, is frequently referred to as an "entrepreneurial ecosystem." While entrepreneurs are the key species in the ecosystem, organizations referred to as Entrepreneurial Support Organizations (ESO) can remove many of the friction points and provide the deep connections for innovators and entrepreneurs to have a much greater chance of success. ESOs bring all of the elements together to build a healthy ecosystem for entrepreneurs to blossom and grow. **A "Startup Junkie" is anyone who works to support and strengthen entrepreneurship in their community.** Also referred to as an "Ecosystem Builder," this person may work in an official ESO, be a civic or business leader, educator, government official, or another form of community champion. This book will cover the elements of a healthy entrepreneurial ecosystem, the role of a Startup Junkie (or Ecosystem Builder), and the secrets to success we have learned while helping entrepreneurship thrive in the heartland.

My name is Jeff Amerine, and I am a Startup Junkie. My team and I embody the entrepreneurial spirit. We are driven by the restlessness of not being satisfied with the way things are done in business and community. This is the story of what it takes to build a successful venture ecosystem in an unexpected place. I am the founder and Managing Director of Startup Junkie, an entrepreneurial support organization located in Fayetteville, Arkansas. I never imagined the business I started 12 years ago would birth a second ecosystem-building brand called the Conductor, located in Conway, Arkansas. These two sides of the same coin are unique in their community culture, local partnerships, and industry specialities. However, both Startup Junkie and Conductor share the same mission of empowering innovators. We believe the key to true economic transformation is to support and grow more entrepreneurs.

My business partner and Managing Director of the Conductor, Dr. Jeff Standridge and I, decided it was time to capture some of our lessons learned about building lasting venture ecosystems in unexpected places like Arkansas. Many members of our teams have made major contributions to this book, and without them, we would have accomplished very little on our journey. If we can make this happen in Arkansas, anyone can make it happen in their locale. Our goal is to give you the insights, lessons learned, and inspiration that help you build a venture ecosystem in your own unexpected and overlooked place.

While we will talk a lot about building sustainable venture ecosystems in your respective communities, we want to be crystal clear about one thing: providing direct support to entrepreneurs and aspiring entrepreneurs is *the primary* purpose of a Startup Junkie and the hallmark of a successful venture ecosystem. There are a lot of activities that go into venture ecosystem building, but Startup Junkies refuse to lose sight of this primary purpose.

What is an entrepreneur?

Simply put, an entrepreneur is someone who starts something, and usually at some degree of financial risk to themselves. The entrepreneurial spirit in the United States is thriving, and small businesses provide the foundation of the U.S. economy. From coffee shops and garages, to Main Street mom-and-pop shops, to eCommerce and cyberspace, entrepreneurs are everywhere you look when searching for the things that matter in your life. Too tired to cook? Try the new all-organic café, Juice Palm. Too tired to shop? Have groceries delivered to your house with no delivery fees from EasyBins. Need to switch up your skincare regimen? Check out a natural face soap like the one created by Heather Urquhart at Hunaskin or by Justin Delaney at Buff City Soap. You can source ingredients for Sunday brunch from an organic farmer like the crew at YeYo's Family Farms or hire a local marketing agency like Dave Creek Media to create your ESO's logo. Perhaps the local school district is looking for an eco-friendly packaging and paper company. Tango-Press has the perfect product to suit their needs. Society abounds with entrepreneurs if you know where to look.

An entrepreneur's contribution to a community benefits everyone. Economic growth leads to lower unemployment and higher wages, which stimulates consumer spending. Gross Domestic Product (GDP) and tax revenues increase, which results in reduced government borrowing and greater investment in schools, roads, and other public services. For every $1 in public money spent on downtown entrepreneurs, $26 in private funds were reinvested back into the community.[1]

In some circles, the word "entrepreneur" conjures a vision of a person who started a high tech, high growth enterprise. In this book, we consider an entrepreneur to be the founder of any venture, big or small, urban or rural, technology-enabled or otherwise. We define "small business" as a venture having 500 employees or less, with annual sales of $750,000 or less, and we define a "startup" as a new small business with high growth potential. The terms "startup" and "small business" will be used interchangeably throughout this book, but both refer to an entrepreneur's development of a new small company. In our experience building a venture ecosystem in Arkansas, we have discovered that supporting small and emerging businesses reaps the biggest social and economic rewards for the community, region, and state.

There are many reasons one may choose to start a business. Some people do so out of *necessity* while others seek *opportunities* to address an unmet market need or demand. Both necessity and opportunity entrepreneurs contribute to economic growth, whether they have one employee or one thousand.[2] For many, being their own boss is tied to the identity and image of living the American Dream.[3] Starting a business allows the average Jane or Joe the opportunity to climb a few rungs on the economic ladder on their own terms.

Small business owners know their communities and their neighbors. They show more concern for the local culture than outsiders or industry giants and have a vested interest in maintaining its vibrancy. As an integral contributor to their community, entrepreneurial businesses improve society by providing locally-made products and services, contributing to the tax base, providing jobs (perhaps for those who are unable to work elsewhere due to commuting or child care restraints), building community with customers and other businesses, and being actively involved beyond the scope of their business as a sponsor for a local sports team or sharing their knowledge and passion with students or local groups.[4]

While historically American entrepreneurs have been white males, the rate of minority-, women-, and veteran-owned businesses is increasing.[5] Inclusive ecosystem building is a targeted approach to reduce barriers to equitable small business ownership,[6] and it helps to support founders who are diverse in gender, age, race, religious or cultural beliefs, education, lifestyle, physical ability, or geographic location.

Why is entrepreneurship important in the United States?

There are over 30 million small businesses in the United States, which accounts for a staggering 99.9% of all U.S. businesses![7] There are many factors that contribute to this high level of entrepreneurship. As a global superpower, the U.S. is a leader in technology[8] and innovation.[9] Venture capital, micro-funding, angel investors and a host of additional options offer a range of funding mechanisms. Entrepreneurial support organizations like the Startup Junkie and Conductor teams run incubators,accelerators and other events and programs that help startups take off. Mentorship programs, associations, and a seemingly infinite range of local, Meetup, and LinkedIn support groups are available at the asking. The country has a diverse population, and businesses enjoy greater freedom in decision making and product development than in many other countries.[10] The entrepreneurial environment is established and welcoming, and the continual expansion to accessible knowledge and ideas promises that entrepreneurs will continue to serve as the foundation of the U.S. economy.

Though most small businesses employ fewer than 20 people, their impact is significant. Entrepreneurs generate 44% of the economy,[11] employ more than 47% of all U.S. workers, and account for 20% of overall job creation.[12] The scope of entrepreneurialism in the U.S is expansive. In 2016, over 400,000 companies engaged in trade, and of those, 97% of importers and 98% of exporters were small or medium-sized enterprises.[13] This translates to over $429 million in exports and nearly $618 million in imports. Not surprisingly, the U.S. is ranked as the top country for entrepreneurs by the Global Economic Development Index[14] and Inc.,[15]and it is among the top three ranked by *U.S. News and World Report*.[16] We couldn't survive without them. Indeed, between 2009 and 2013, as the United States was slowly recovering from recession, 60% of jobs were created by small businesses.[17] As magnified by the U.S. recession of 2020, it is vital that ecosystem builders continue to nurture and grow small businesses.[18]

What are some challenges to entrepreneurship?

While becoming an entrepreneur has many benefits, it is not fail-proof. Many new businesses don't survive – only about half last for five or more years, and about a third will make it until their tenth year. New startups also are more sensitive to the economic environment and business cycles. The Great Recession that started in the early 2000s took a toll on the nation's entrepreneurial spirit and recovery has been slow.[19] The number of new businesses being started is at its lowest point since the late-1980s,[20] compounded by the negative impact of COVID-19.

However, for most entrepreneurs the success of a new business is not tied to the status of the economy or even the presence of a global pandemic. Most (42%) startups fail because they created a product or service that no one wanted. This puts the business at a disadvantage from the start with the domino effect of inadequate cash flow and forced downsizing of employees. [21] ESOs can help entrepreneurs in these critical early stages by helping with customer discovery and identifying product-market fit. Ecosystem Builders also serve as trusted advisors, technical assistance providers, and oftentimes a source of encouragement. When a founder is feeling frustrated, Ecosystem Builders can remind them that entrepreneurs who had a previous business, whether successful or not, are 20-30% more likely to be successful with the next venture. ESOs can also provide networking functions to encourage new relationships and opportunities for entrepreneurs to meet potential co-founders. ESOs serve as the catalyst for new ideas, new connections, and new possibilities. Entrepreneurship is hard work, which is why having a thriving ecosystem can help make or break the success of local small businesses. The Startup Junkie and Conductor teams have seen this first hand and can attest to the difference ESOs can make in ensuring entrepreneurs are victorious in their quest to start the next best company.

What is the current state of entrepreneurship globally?

Entrepreneurship is alive and flourishing throughout the world. Developed countries like Switzerland, the United Kingdom, and Australia are top-rated for their entrepreneurialism.[22] These countries lead the world in wealth, educational opportunities, and technological advances. However, smaller countries with less access to support resources also have high levels of entrepreneurship. The Netherlands, Israel, Chile, and Belgium rank among the Top 20 entrepreneurial countries by both the Global Entrepreneurship Index (GEI) and the Global Entrepreneurship Monitor (GEM).[23] The Netherlands and Israel, along with Estonia, Cyprus, and Luxembourg, are leaders among innovation-driven countries. Estonia and Israel also hold the number one and two ranking, respectively, for their level of entrepreneurial employee activity. Luxemburg and Chile have the highest innovation levels.[24] Other countries also stand out for their unique strengths. For example, Iceland has the highest rating for entrepreneurial attitude, which indicates a country's recognition and support for entrepreneurs, and Switzerland leads in both entrepreneurial abilities and aspirations.[25] With limited job prospects, citizens of smaller countries have no alternative but to embrace an entrepreneurial attitude. Despite weak infrastructure, minimal or no financing, unreliable access to the internet and other technologies, and no support from ESOs, these innovators use whatever means available to provide for themselves and their families, like selling homemade food or goods or providing services as drivers or tour guides.

What are some countries that demonstrate entrepreneurial leadership?

Every country has their own unique circumstances that inspire its particular brand of entrepreneurism. Ten years after the publication of *Startup Nation: The Story of Israel's Economic Miracle*, Israel continues to live up to their reputation of being a hotbed of entrepreneurial activity. Several factors contribute to the success of this New Jersey-sized country. As a small country with limited natural resources and a limited domestic market, entrepreneurs must look to exports and be innovative in creating new value.[26] Israel also spends more on research and development as a percentage of gross domestic product than any other country. That said, because they are a small country, contacts are easy to make through existing networks. Perhaps most important is their perseverance, born from centuries of struggle. As Dan Senior and Saul Singer, authors of *Startup Nation*, put it, Israelis have *chutzpah*, that is, audacity or nerve.[27] It is this attitude of boldness and confidence that keeps them determined to foster entrepreneurial spirit. To make sure the rest of the world knows their success, they invite select entrepreneurs and journalists from other countries to meet and study its startup secrets.

In Chile, the government created a public startup accelerator, Start-up Chile, to encourage entrepreneurship on a nation-wide scale. Today, it is among the biggest and most diverse accelerators in the world. It offers different programs based on the idea being developed and the stage of development, as well as specific programming for women. To date they have helped more than 1,600 startups that have contributed to economic, social, and cultural impact, while inspiring and influencing more than 50 other countries to create similar programs.[28]

India is taking a multifaceted approach to supporting entrepreneurs at T-Hub in Hyderabad. Branded as an Innovation Ecosystem, T-Hub leverages and connects leadership from industry, government, startups, and venture capital to meet entrepreneurs at any stage of development and provide them a roadmap to grow. They have assisted more than 550 startups, hosted over 850 events, and raised more than $186M since opening in 2015.[29]

What these exemplary countries have in common is a robust venture ecosystem that exists to support and grow entrepreneurs. These ecosystems are unique to the local culture, talent, and market opportunities. These countries, and many others who may be considered forerunners of entrepreneurialism, are the backbone of a thriving global entrepreneurial community. Their innovations and new products contribute to a more robust economy and job options for their citizens. Global entrepreneurialism succeeds when there is an ecosystem of interconnected and supported components. This means access to technology, financing, a legal and regulatory structure, skilled workers, mentorship, and support. When the level of entrepreneurship is productive and scalable, it benefits not only the entrepreneur, but also the community, region, state, country, and world!

CHAPTER 2:

What is an Entrepreneurial Ecosystem?

When did the "Entrepreneurial Movement" begin?

The United States has long favored and rewarded innovation. George Washington is credited with being the first entrepreneur, and as "Executive-in-Chief" he certainly demonstrated impressive business acumen. He paid down the equivalent of trillions of dollars in international debt by creating a national bank and establishing a currency. This built the nation's credit and established an economic system that served as the foundation for future presidents.[30]

A close friend of Washington, Ben Franklin, is renowned for his inventions and entrepreneurial spirit. He perceived demands and sought to fill them. Among his eclectic inventions are the lightning rod, bifocal glasses, streetlamps, catheters, and swim fins; he also conceived of and started the concept of franchising.[31] Franklin's ideas rewarded him in spirit and finance, allowing him to retire from business at the age of 42. Characteristic of his commitment to progress, he never patented any of his work. Instead, he believed that everyone should be able to benefit from their use and felt that inventors should "freely and generously" share the advantages they bring.[32]

The expansion of railroad and communication systems in the 19th century opened a new world of possibilities. Thomas Edison, another publisher and inventor, picked up Franklin's torch and developed several telegraphic and electric inventions that are either still in use or serve as the model for newer versions. In addition to his well-known contributions like the lightbulb and phonograph, Edison also created the kinetoscope for motion pictures, an electric pen, a mimeograph microtasimeter (used to measure minute changes in temperature), and a method for wireless telegraphy used heavily by railway systems.[33] It was the success of Edison and other visionaries of that time, such as Andrew Carnegie and Henry Ford, that encouraged financiers and capitalists to provide funding for these types of innovative projects.[34]

The more recent trend in entrepreneurialism grew from the tech wave that started in the 1970s with the start of Microsoft and Apple and exploded in the 1990s and the early part of this century. Microsoft founder Bill Gates and Apple founder Steve Jobs became and remain the faces that represent the marriage of technology and entrepreneurialism. By 2010, Apple was dominating computer sales, having already changed the world of music with the introduction of their iPod media player and the iPhone. During this time, we were introduced to Google, LinkedIn, Instacart, Spotify, and Canva - all changing the way we live and do business.

However, not all revolutionary innovations utilize a power switch, as entrepreneurialism has been the solution to many of life's challenges. In the late 1800s, Madam C.J. Walker, after years of struggle with hair loss, invented the first specialized haircare system for African American women. Called the "Walker System of Beauty Culture," this invention not only revolutionized the natural hair industry, but also changed the approach of direct sales. Walker utilized "beauty culturists" who lived all across the United States and could personally testify to her product's effectiveness.[35]

Another entrepreneur born from necessity, Sara Blakely first realized the need for specialized women's undergarments when she cut the feet out of a pair of pantyhose to have a seamless silhouette in business trousers. The success of her shapewear brand Spanx has taken her from door-to-door fax salesperson to a $1 billion dollar clothing mogul, part owner of a basketball team, and judge on the television show "Shark Tank," which has helped bring entrepreneurs and their stories into the mainstream media discussion.[36] Fellow Shark Tank judge Daymond John has been able to transcend typical industry silos and expanded his successful ventures in multiple markets. A modern serial entrepreneur, John started his clothing company FUBU in the early 1990s in his mother's house. Thirty years later, FUBU has topped $6 billion in global sales, and John now includes investor, author, and motivational speaker to his list of accomplishments.[37]

As time progressed and innovations became more complex, so did the systems required to support such radical ventures. Beyond only needing customers to survive, entrepreneurs need to know how to file appropriate incorporation documents, patent applications, or lending forms. They need to know how to market their product, or who to hire to help. They need capital, developers, storefronts, CPAs, eCommerce capabilities, lawyers, mentors, and other resources to help take their ideas to market. Three hundred years ago Benjamin Franklin could only rely on his wit and curiosity to spark life into his inventions. Today, entrepreneurs can count on their entrepreneurial ecosystem to support them on their innovation journey.

What is an entrepreneurial ecosystem?

Critical to the success of entrepreneurship is a healthy entrepreneurial ecosystem. Formally defined as "a set of interdependent actors and factors coordinated in such a way that they enable productive entrepreneurship within a particular territory,"[38] entrepreneurial ecosystems provide a framework that makes available the resources necessary for entrepreneurs to start and grow their businesses.

Consider the metaphors of recipes and production to describe this ecosystem. Entrepreneurs try new combinations (i.e., using different "ingredients") that create production recipes, and the outputs result from a set of specific, distinct steps used to create the recipe. Entrepreneurship is trying out the production recipes.[39] Some are excellent and are used over and over; others are one-and-done. For example, a new small coffee/sandwich business may open at a train station to cater to rush-hour customers. However, the neighbors take note and start stopping by, so the owner adds additional menu items. Recognizing the untapped market of the senior home down the block, card games and book clubs are added to the afternoon calendar. Trying different combinations to get to the best mix led to a new production recipe. This "recipe" filled a food and social gap in the area, maximized use of the shop's resources, and added a productive new startup to the community.

There are many descriptions of what an entrepreneurial ecosystem is and how it is measured, but they all share several common elements: [40]

Human Capital: The availability of skilled and unskilled labor, high-school and college students, and training program graduates. A highly knowledgeable STEM based workforce is even better.

Culture: An environment that is tolerant of risks and mistakes and one that embraces innovation.

Finance: Access to a range of funding options, including banks, government agencies, grants, venture capital, angels, and micro loans.

Markets: Domestic and international corporations, consumers, and distribution and marketing networks to create and fill demand.

Policies: Structure created by established and reasonable tax rates, a regulatory framework, and incentives for doing business.

Support: Infrastructure support (e.g., utilities, communications, transportation) and business support (e.g., legal and accounting advisers, technical advisors, mentors, incubators and accelerators).

The concept of an ecosystem to support entrepreneurs is still evolving. Although this approach has been used for more than twenty years, there are still areas that need to be more consistently established for a broader universal acceptance and implementation, such as common measures, methods, terminology, and outcomes.[41]

In addition to providing a starting point for new entrepreneurs, a strong ecosystem also helps to guide entrepreneurs as they navigate through new technologies, economies, and changes. An entrepreneur who starts a business out of necessity might shift direction to focus on the aspect of the business that offers the greatest potential to become an opportunity entrepreneur. The structure and support offered by an entrepreneurial ecosystem allows entrepreneurs to move from idea to realization.

Lastly, strong ecosystems have frequent and consistent storytelling, shaping the narrative of a vibrant entrepreneurial environment while highlighting local successes. Storytelling creates momentum within a community and informs external stakeholders about progress and business opportunities. Clear and frequent messaging is vital to cultivating an environment that is open to risk taking and innovation.[42]

Who are some of the major players in the Ecosystem-building Movement?

Many organizations have been instrumental in creating and promoting entrepreneurial ecosystems that help build sustainable, successful businesses. Some of the bigger players in this space include:

Ewing Marion Kauffman Foundation – Considered by many to be the powerhouse of this group, the Kauffman Foundation supports many key initiatives for entrepreneurs from educational opportunities to policy change.[43]

Babson Entrepreneurship Ecosystem Project (BEEP) – BEEP offers resources to help leaders create cultures, policies, programs, and structures that foster entrepreneurship.[44]

Entrepreneurs Organization – This global network of entrepreneurs hosts regional and global forums and events, including student entrepreneur awards. They also offer an accelerator program and provide executive education to serve the "complete" entrepreneur.[45]

Global Entrepreneur Network (GEN) - GEN works to start and grow ecosystems by encouraging world-wide collaboration and initiatives between entrepreneurial stakeholders to increase economic, educational, innovation, and inclusive activities.[46]

Tugboat Institute – Tugboat focuses on "evergreen" businesses: purpose-driven leaders looking to make a long-term positive impact in the world.[47]

The Case Foundation - Created in 1997, The Case Foundation drives social change based on the pillars of revolutionizing philanthropy, unleashing entrepreneurs, and igniting civic engagement.[48]

Main Street America - With a targeted focus on "downtown" ventures, Main Street America provides individualized technical assistance to support entrepreneurs in commercial districts. They also provide ecosystem analysis tools for municipal leaders to support economic development efforts that prioritize entrepreneurship.[49]

InBIA - This non-profit supports a global network for entrepreneurial support organizations, including incubators, university centers, accelerators, and government programs with a shared vision of supporting inclusive entrepreneurial development.[50]

What is an Entrepreneurial Support Organization (ESO)?

Entrepreneurs can also find support to grow their business through the hundreds of Entrepreneurial Support Organizations (ESO) established throughout the country. These organizations take many forms and cater to virtually any category with which an entrepreneur might identify: age, gender, industry, business size, revenue, product or service, geographic region, and more.

While some corporations offer entrepreneurial programs for employees, or "intrapreneurs,"[51] most ESOs are nonprofit or university-affiliated. Their function is to help entrepreneurs make the most of the resources they have. Nonprofit ESOs generally receive funding from the government and generate any additional income through a revenue stream (e.g., offering classes) or individual donations. University ESOs are similar in function but reside within a university which allows them to make use of faculty and student resources to support the organization.[52] Universities also provide an excellent platform for developing entrepreneurs. Diverse groups of ambitious, high-achieving students are co-located, thereby creating the ideal environment for innovation. They have access to the latest technologies and resources, and they have a high tolerance for risk.[53] The next greatest thing we can't live without may be in someone's dorm room at this moment!

Incubators and accelerators are examples of ESOs, as are innovation labs, associations, and various other entities. Incubators provide support at the startup of a business when the idea or maybe even a prototype exists, but there is no business plan or model to bring it to reality. Co-working and shared spaces are hallmarks of incubators, and while some incubators may take a small amount of equity, most do not. Entrepreneurs who are accepted into an incubator program may be required to relocate so that participants can benefit from each other's ideas and their networks, mentorship, and the community in which they are located. Because incubators focus on developing and refining the idea to ensure success, they work at their own pace without a defined timeline.[54]

Accelerators, as the name suggests, are designed to accelerate a business. Unlike incubators, accelerators are structured and take place within a specific timeframe, which could be weeks or months. The goal of accelerators is to increase the size and value of a business quickly to prepare it for an initial round of funding. To do this, some accelerators provide a seed investment in exchange for a small equity stake in the business. Accelerators also offer an extensive network of mentors, industry specialists, startup executives, venture capitalists, and other investors. These extremely competitive programs look for startups that can show rapid growth and are scalable and investable. Because of the advantages these opportunities offer, top programs generally accept a small percentage of the many applicants they receive.[55]

There are pros and cons for entrepreneurs to work with incubators and accelerators. On the plus side, they provide new entrepreneurs with access to information and ideas, mentorship, and a valuable professional network. These critical connections offer much needed access to funders and can help identify costly and irreversible mistakes before they happen. Conversely, some entrepreneurs feel that working with others can be distracting or diminishes creativity. Also, when an entrepreneur accepts a spot in an accelerator program that requires a time commitment, they may have to change or give up elements of their idea.[56] Part of being an effective ecosystem builder is understanding the different programs available and helping an entrepreneur find a fit that is right for them.

While most ESOs are locally focused, there are many who are quickly gaining national attention. Here are just a few representative examples:

Dreamit Ventures: Dreamit is an accelerator for startups creating "transformative tech" in healthcare, real estate, and security environments.[57]

CO.STARTERS: With a primary focus on strengthening communities, CO.STARTERS provides local leaders with a framework to grow new entrepreneurs and support existing small businesses.[58]

Idealab: A technology incubator, Idealab has created over 150 companies with more than 45 IPOs and acquisitions.[59]

StartupNation: This multimedia company creates content by and for entrepreneurs to start, grow, and manage a business.[60]

Techstars: A global accelerator, Techstars focuses on web-based and software companies but also considers unique projects.[61]

Y-Combinator: A seed accelerator, Y-Combinators funds different types of projects during the two sessions it hosts each year.

Black Girl Ventures: This multi-city organization aims to democratize entrepreneurship for black and brown women by connecting them to social and financial capital and preparing them to participate in accelerator programs.[62]

Center on Rural Innovation: This network of rural innovation hubs provides support to enhance innovation in rural communities by supplying a GIS enabled Opportunity Map highlighting opportunity zones across the nation and the CORI Innovation Fund for entrepreneurs in opportunity zones.[63]

Forward Cities: Founded in 2014, this multi-city collaborative utilizes the Equitable Entrepreneurial Ecosystem (E3) program to provide an inclusive entrepreneurial learning network for member communities to grow more entrepreneurs.[64]

Young Entrepreneur Council: This is an invitation-only forum for young (under 45) entrepreneurs to provide mentorship, exchange ideas and resources, and develop their connections.[65]

Startup Junkie: An Arkansas-based, no-cost comprehensive entrepreneurial support organization helping entrepreneurs expand the reach, impact, and depth of their services.[66]

The Conductor: A public-private partnership between Startup Junkie and the University of Central Arkansas to drive innovation, entrepreneurship, and economic empowerment in Central Arkansas.[67]

As entrepreneurial support organizations continue to grow and influence traditional economic development strategies, specialized conferences and professional development opportunities are becoming available for ecosystem builders looking to expand their knowledge, skills, and relationships. The Kauffman ESHIP Summit, Tom Tom Festival, Rural Rise, and Startup Champions are a few annual celebrations with a specific focus on ecosystem building. Entrepreneurs themselves have taken notice of this movement, with tech titans Brad Feld, Victor Hwang, and Steve Case becoming outspoken advocates of ecosystem building as they travel across America promoting their research on the subject. At Startup Junkie and the Conductor, we work closely with our colleagues at Chambers of Commerce, universities, nonprofits, municipalities, and other ESOs to increase entrepreneurship in the heartland. Whether you are an experienced ecosystem builder or are just beginning your startup champion journey, there are unlimited op-

tions to plug in and gain the tools to best serve the entrepreneurs in your community.

CHAPTER 3:

Entrepreneurship in the US "Flyover States"

When most people think of a vibrant entrepreneurial ecosystem, big bustling cities come to mind. Many of the places shown in the media that have cutting-edge reputations like New York, Los Angeles, or Miami are often advertised as being the destination of choice for innovators and entrepreneurs. While the coastal states of the U.S. certainly do offer some startup amenities, the true land of entrepreneurial opportunity is actually right in the middle, the most "flown over" parts of the country.

What are the flyover states?

The term "flyover states" refers to everything between New York and California, and these states are the heart of the country.[68] They are north and south, small and large, urban and rural. Their cities and towns are increasingly diverse and rich with unique customs and traditions that reflect the values and openness of their residents. Flyover states offer many of the benefits of big cities – jobs, culture, access – without the frenetic pace and high cost of living.

49

West Virginia has the distinction of being, literally, the most flown over state. In fact, there are 195 more flights that go *over* West Virginia than land there as a destination. Other major "flyovers" include Kansas, Mississippi, Iowa, Kentucky, Wyoming, New Mexico, Arkansas, Alabama, South Dakota, Nebraska, Idaho, Montana, North Dakota, Oklahoma, Indiana, Utah, Colorado, and Missouri. [69]

What are some of the population and economic statistics of the flyover states?[70]

The average and median salaries in these states tend to be lower than the U.S. average, though the majority of them (14) also have lower than average unemployment rates. Similarly, the sales tax in fourteen of these states is lower than the national average.

Conversely, many flyover states are paying more than their fair share of taxes with roughly 70% of them having higher than average income tax rates (though it should be noted that South Dakota and Wyoming have no income tax). Among the flyover states, Utah, Colorado, Indiana, Kentucky, and Idaho stand out in terms of projected 10-year job growth. Idaho tied with Nevada as the fastest growing state in 2018.[71]

Living in these states offers many advantages. Housing and cost of living are lower, and the quality of life is higher. The people are educated and patient with a strong work ethic. This means a talented workforce is at the ready. The centrality of these states offers closer proximity to suppliers and customers, and financial incentives for new businesses make them increasingly desirable. The available resources makes these places prime locations for a thriving venture ecosystem. For example, Hamilton County in Indiana offers a great school system, a low cost of living, and access to major freeways. Thanks to its strong manufacturing sector, it is becoming one of the fastest growing and most business-friendly counties in the country.[72]

The table below identifies population and economic characteristics of the flyover states that make them a desirable location for entrepreneurs to start a business.

	2018 Population	Unemployment Rate	Expected 10-yr Job Growth	Average Income	Median Income	Sales Tax	Income Tax Rate
Indiana	6,691,878	3.4%	34.8%	$ 24,953	$ 48,737	7.0%	3.2%
Missourri	6,126,452	3.3%	27.3%	$ 26,006	$ 47,764	7.7%	5.9%
Colorado	5,695,564	3.1%	46.0%	$ 31,674	$ 59,448	7.2%	4.6%
Alabama	4,887,871	4.0%	32.4%	$ 23,936	$ 43,511	8.4%	5.0%
Kentucky	4,468,402	4.3%	34.9%	$ 23,741	$ 43,342	6.0%	5.8%
Oklahoma	3,943,079	3.6%	28.9%	$ 24,695	$ 45,235	8.4%	5.0%
Utah	3,161,105	3.1%	42.9%	$ 24,312	$ 59,846	6.8%	5.0%
Iowa	3,156,145	2.5%	26.8%	$ 27,621	$ 52,716	6.8%	9.0%
Arkansas	3,013,825	3.7%	29.8%	$ 22,595	$ 28,555	7.3%	4.6%
Mississippi	2,986,530	4.7%	29.3%	$ 20,956	$ 39,464	7.1%	5.0%
Kansas	2,911,505	3.3%	25.7%	$ 27,367	$ 51,872	8.6%	5.7%
New Mexico	2,095,428	4.9%	29.4%	$ 23,948	$ 44,968	7.5%	4.9%
Nebraska	1,929,268	2.8%	28.2%	$ 27,339	$ 52,400	6.7%	6.8%
West Virginia	1,805,832	5.2%	26.0%	$ 23,237	$ 41,756	6.2%	6.5%
Idaho	1,754,208	2.8%	43.8%	$ 23,087	$ 47,334	6.0%	7.4%
Montana	1,062,305	3.8%	28.2%	$ 25,977	$ 46,766	0.0%	6.9%
South Dakota	882,235	3.1%	29.8%	$ 26,311	$ 50,338	6.0%	0%
North Dakota	760,077	2.7%	22.2%	$ 30,894	$ 55,579	6.7%	2.0%
Wyoming	577,737	3.9%	13.3%	$ 29,381	$ 58,252	5.5%	0%
US AVG		**3.6%**	**30.5%**	**$ 25,531**	**$ 47,957**	**6.6%**	**4.9%**

Why do entrepreneurial ecosystems matter in flyover states?

Silicon Valley has long been considered the end-all, be-all of technology and innovation. Few people go through a day without the help of Google or YouTube, which they access through a Microsoft or Apple system. The founding fathers of tech innovation became the beacon for start-ups, drawing an influx of great minds (and full wallets) to the Bay Area. Certainly this recognition is well-deserved, but this epicenter of entrepreneurial spirit no longer stands alone in the spotlight.

The very technologies created by this entrepreneurial stronghold now make it possible for entrepreneurs virtually anywhere in the world access customers, suppliers, competitors, peers, mentors, research, and a wealth of other resources across the globe. The world has become a connected and inviting place, welcoming of new and never-before-considered ideas, and many of these ideas are emerging from the flyover states.

The flyover states also offer a host of incentives to contribute to a healthy venture ecosystem. The lower cost of living means more affordable office or work space, as well as comfortable homes for employees. Advances in technology, such as cloud computing and the portability of social networks, further contribute to lower costs. Universities and other accelerator programs are already established and provide a local support infrastructure. Furthermore, access to capital is increasingly available. In addition to crowd-funding, more angel investors and venture capitalists are looking beyond New York and California to see what's new and interesting in the rest of the country.[73]

The cost of living in the flyover states is a big draw in attracting those who want more bang for their creative and investment buck. The lifestyle draws them in and the opportunities keep them. Of note, the innovations and ideas coming from the center states often differ from the nearly exclusive tech-focus of Silicon Valley. Entrepreneurs in middle America evolve and develop innovations that solve real-life problems for their communities. In stark contrast to the "strike it rich quick" mindset that created – and burst – the dot com bubble on both coasts, the patience synonymous with the states in flyover territory is an asset in developing relationships and partnerships. Unlike their west coast counterparts, entrepreneurs in flyover states aren't looking to create a business, sell it, and then take that

$100 million and start something new. Instead, they set out to address a challenge and develop realistic expectations about developing and scaling their business to meet that challenge. [74]

There is tremendous support for building a stronger entrepreneurial infrastructure throughout the country. AOL founder Steve Case joined forces with best-selling author J.D. Vance to create Revolution, their own startup that invests in "people and ideas that change the world." Their focus is exclusively outside of Silicon Valley, New York, and Boston. Taking a lead from politicians and rock bands, they outfitted a bus and took it across the country, hosting entrepreneurship competitions at which participants were eligible to win $100,000 in seed money for their idea. Case and Vance collected a Who's Who of investors, including Jeff Bezos (Amazon), the Waltons (Walmart), Howard Schultz (Starbucks), and a host of other billionaire investors and entrepreneurs to support their project. Their goal is to provide seed money to help startups get established in underrepresented cities, and then bring in the big money investors for the second round.

Efforts such as these are becoming more common and foster the growth of new pockets of entrepreneurship all over the country. This momentum must continue in order to accelerate entrepreneurship in all 50 states. Local business and civic leaders must encourage opportunities and support initiatives in their communities and at their universities through accelerators and other programs. Creating thriving ecosystems throughout the country will not only benefit communities throughout the United States, but also further ensure our competitive edge in the increasingly growing global economy.[75]

What are some flyover states with successful entrepreneurial ecosystems?

Utah

It is almost impossible to talk about anything entrepreneur-related without mentioning Utah. Known for its innovative culture, it offers established networks, government leadership, and risk capital. In 2014, Utah led the country in dollar-per-deal averages, beating San Francisco by nearly $33 million. The University of Utah and Utah State University house incubators for technology inventions, and the state government's Utah Science Technology and Research Initiative provides further support by funding research, risk capital, and the talent pipeline.[76] Provo, for example, is home of Brigham Young University and consistently ranks as having a high quality of life. It has a highly educated workforce, low cost of living, and proximity to amazing skiing and outdoor recreation, making it a desired alternative for those leaving behind the high costs of Silicon Valley.

Nebraska

The citizens of Omaha have known for a long time that they are an entrepreneurial ecosystem – it just took a little while for everyone else to catch on. Now that they have, there is no limit to what can happen there. A growing city that manages to retain the feel of a small community, Omaha was voted as the best place in America to work in tech (2014), and it continues to be included among the best cities for entrepreneurs.[77] Like other flyover cities, entrepreneurs in Omaha are not out for the thrill of a quick sale: they support their communities and each other.[78] Not only do they have access to the checklist of entrepreneurial resources (accelerators, funding, a start-up collaborative, and a pipeline of talent), they also boast culture, great food, and North America's largest indoor rainforest.[79]

Oklahoma

In addition to being a great environment for entrepreneurs overall, Tulsa has made a determined effort to create opportunities for underrepresented groups. A 2016 survey included Tulsa as the best city in the United States for women to start a business, and WalletHub listed it as 12th on the list of best cities for Hispanic entrepreneurs. It is home to an enviable number of incubators, coworking spaces, accelerators, and makerspaces with several angel and venture capital investors who focus specifically on start-ups in and around Oklahoma. They also host a variety of entrepreneurial events, including a Women's Leadership Summit and competitions for startups.[80]

Minnesota

In 2018, Business.org included Minneapolis and St. Paul in their top three cities for entrepreneurs and startups. Minneapolis had the highest startup growth among the top ten cities at 121%.[81] TechCrunch lists Minneapolis as the 2nd best startup city in the Midwest overall, in the number of startups founded, and in the number of investment rounds and venture capital deals.[82] This isn't surprising to the entrepreneurs of the Twin Cities who saw a 40% increase in startup investments between 2016 and 2017, no doubt due in part to the collegiality among the businesses located there.[83] Innovations in Minnesota tend to focus on food and agriculture, health care, and enterprise-level business-to-business solutions.[84] To ensure their continued inclusion among the best and brightest in entrepreneurship, the newly elected mayors of both Sister Cities are staunch supporters of entrepreneurship and have committed to providing resources necessary for the success of their start-ups, including the launch of a new Small Business Portal.[85] The cost of living is low but tech pay is nearly twice as high as the state's average wages, which affords residents the opportunity to take advantage of the art, culture, and other attractions in the region.

Arkansas

The home of legendary founders Sam Walton (Walmart), John Tyson (Tyson Foods) and Johnnie Bryan Hunt (J.B. Hunt Transport Services), Arkansas has entrepreneurship in it's blood. All three of these companies are headquartered in the Northwest corner of the state, which has become a hub for startup activity, in part due to the leadership of entrepreneurial support organizations like Startup Junkie. With a decade of experience and roots in university tech transfer, we host programming like the FUEL Accelerator for startups in the Artificial Intelligence space and have a top-reviewed entrepreneurial podcast with downloads from across the globe.[86] We also have an ecosystem hub in the central part of the state under the brand the Conductor. A public-private partnership with the University of Central Arkansas, the Conductor coordinates the 10x Accelerator for tech-enabled high growth companies and has expertise in healthcare innovation, data analytics, and angel investing. Through the creation of the Venture Ecosystem Building Canvas, the Conductor takes a holistic approach to ecosystem building, working closely with community leaders and policymakers on creating lasting, sustainable change. In addition to Startup Junkie and the Conductor, the State of Arkansas also benefits from the work of the Venture Center, HealthTech Arkansas, and Innovate Arkansas, each located in Little Rock; the Arkansas Regional Innovation Hub, located in North Little

Rock; A-State Innovate, located in Jonesboro; the Women's Business Center, located in Eldorado; a network of Small Business and Technology Development Centers located around the state, and other individuals, programs, organizations, and institutions who work together to support entrepreneurial activity in various forms.

Idaho

Dubbed the "Next Silicon Valley" by *Inc. Magazine*,[87] Boise is quickly becoming a destination location for founders and startups. Boise is number five on Inc.'s Top 50 List of best cities to start a business beating out tech giant San Francisco.[88] With a low cost of living and high business leadership engagement, Boise has raised over $70M in venture capital in the last five years. During this time, Boise State University created Venture College, a university initiative to encourage entrepreneurship. Coworking and innovation spaces have also sprung up around the city, fostering a culture of collaboration and discovery.[89] Boise also takes particular care to empower entrepreneurs from under-supported groups with the Idaho Hispanic Foundation, which hosts the Idaho Women's Business Center in partnership with the US. Small Business Administration.[90]

Tennessee

The home of Chattanooga, the first city in America to have high internet available to all of its residents (current speed is 10GB/second), Tennessee is a great place to start a tech enabled company.[91] Chattanooga also houses Tennessee's largest incubator with 127,000 square feet of space dedicated to supporting entrepreneurs.[92] The western part of the state is home to Epicenter Memphis, a coworking and networking space dedicated to inclusive entrepreneurship.[93] Another organization dedicated to equitable access to startup support is Start Co., which provides mentorship and an accelerator program to Delta area entrepreneurs.[94] Both of these organizations are participants in the 800 Initiative, a movement to increase minority venture capital investment in the city of Memphis by $50M in the next five years.[95]

All of these flyover states are unique in their assets and characteristics, offering different strengths and resources to the multitude of entrepreneurs who call the region home. The one element they all share is the special support structure that venture ecosystems in the heartland need to thrive - a solid foundation built on the four pillars of talent, culture, community engagement, and capital.

PART 2:

The Four Pillars of Ecosystem Building

CHAPTER 4:

Talent

A s we shared in Chapter 1, there are many document-ed factors that contribute to an entrepreneurial eco-system, including the availability of skilled and unskilled labor; a collaborative environment that is tolerant of risks and mistakes and embraces innovation; access to a range of funding options; established and reasonable public policy; and a solid and supportive infrastructure. How these areas are displayed looks different in every ecosystem because of the diverse people and opportunities available in each re-gion. The Startup Junkie and Conductor teams have seen how unique communities and entrepreneurs can be even within the same state. Because of this variety of resources, we have identified four overarching pillars that encompass the many factors that work together for an ecosystem to function. From our experience, the strength of these four pillars determines the overall health and longevity of a ven-ture ecosystem in the heartland.

What are the four pillars of venture ecosystem building?

The four pillars that provide the structure and support for the rest of the entrepreneurial ecosystem are talent, culture, community engagement, and capital.

Talent:

A talented workforce is unquestionably the most important element in the ecosystem. This starts with the entrepreneurs themselves and extends to those who join them, not only the employees but also the mentors and advisors who guide them. Smart, ambitious, passionate people who are excited by risk and opportunity are attracted to the entrepreneurial culture, and they are central to the success of any business venture. This isn't the first time we've said this, and it won't be the last.

Culture:

Entrepreneurship requires the appetite to try something new and the bravery to continue even after failure. An entrepreneurial culture should embrace the same spirit of risk-taking and exploration. The culture should appreciate and celebrate people who are innovative, determined, confident, disciplined, and open-minded self-starters. This collaborative culture is reflected in the way municipal leaders make decisions, government officials set policies, and industry titans invest their time and resources. The culture of the wider ecosystem influences the startups within them.

Community Engagement:

Common interests, goals, attitudes, and a sense of fellowship characterize communities. Entrepreneurial ecosystems epitomize and elevate the concept of community through a systemic approach to identifying, developing, funding, and sustaining entrepreneurship. This emphasis on interdependence across all factors in the system keeps the cycle alive and flourishing as new entrepreneurs are drawn to the community by the value of its talent, capital, and culture. Key actors in an engaged community are flagship enterprises, public institutions, local government, and the general public. Culture is what prompts an entrepreneur to start a business. Community Engagement is what helps the business grow.

Capital:

Following closely behind talented human capital is financial capital. While some entrepreneurs are in the position to fund their own startups, most are not. Capital can be in the form of venture funding, SBA backed commercial loans, CDFI microloans, or crowdsourced monies. Regardless of where the funds come from, an ecosystem must have capital available and be able to tell an entrepreneur where to find it.

What role does talent play in building out an ecosystem?

One of the most exciting things about the entrepreneurial ecosystem is seeing ingenuity and creativity as unique ideas come to life. What starts out as a thought becomes a tangible product or service that can become recognized and appreciated by ten or ten thousand users. Critical to this transformation is fostering an environment that attracts the right people to make the dream a reality.

The term "talent" is a great way to describe entrepreneurship because it takes a special gift to bring one's goals to life. Entrepreneurs also need an experienced and talented team to help fill the gaps in areas where their own skills may be lacking, such as record-keeping or marketing. An ecosystem needs to support the development of both kinds of talent - the entrepreneurs themselves and the experts who help their companies grow.

Access to high-level talent is foundational to any entrepreneurial ecosystem, and some communities do a really outstanding job of recognizing the value of their talent as the heartbeat to the system. For example, Texas has been the lone star on several entrepreneurial indices, representing four of the top ten cities with startup activity in the 2017 Kauffman Index of Startup Activity (they also had the 11th ranked city!).[96] A contributing factor is the nature of the people who display solid teamwork and excellent customer service.[97] Texans are hard-working and among the most productive people in the country.[98] Texas has a good representation of STEM workers and is also ranked as the number one state for women entrepreneurs.[99] Austin is cited as one of the best cities to build a startup.[100] Is it any surprise that Texas has the third highest growth rate in the country?[101]

Colorado has one of the best-educated workforces in the U.S. and a strong worker training program. They also have a strong STEM alliance of business, education, and civic leaders that strive to create a new generation of high-tech workers.[102] Denver and Boulder in particular are havens for startups. In Boulder, 15% of all jobs are STEM-related; only San Jose has a higher ranking.[103]Aurora, Lakewood, and Fort Collins are also rising stars with an abundance of tech companies, affordable housing, and high income households.[104]

Detroit and Ann Arbor put Michigan on the map for talent development. Ann Arbor, home to the University of Michigan, was ranked as the most-educated city in the world. The Kauffman Foundation ranked it 13th in established small business activity, 15th for startup activity, and 25th for entrepreneurial growth.[105] Just fifty miles east, Detroit experienced a 54% increase in the number of city-based venture-backed startups between 2014 and 2018, and 56% of venture capital was invested in information technology startups in 2017. Michigan has one of the highest concentrations of STEM workers[106] and the highest density of engineers in the U.S.[107]

What role should universities play in developing ecosystems?

Universities are some of the primary producers of entrepreneurial talent. Even though many of the most famous entrepreneurs never graduated from college, including Steve Jobs, Bill Gates, and Mark Zuckerberg, more than 90% of tech founders have a college degree.[108] College isn't for everyone, but having a college in the local community contributes to a culture of learning, curiosity, and complex problem solving.

In and of themselves, universities can serve as a hub for highly skilled and specialized talent. There is a circular effect as the brightest minds seek institutions that support their goals and, in turn, the institution produces graduate entrepreneurs who contribute to the community – there or elsewhere – providing opportunities for other great minds. College is also a place where entrepreneurs often build life-long relationships and meet potential partners, funders, and customers.

Some universities serve in a boundary-spanning role. That is, they are influenced by the specific region and innovations of their location (e.g., Minnesota is a hub for food and agriculture), and in turn they provide reciprocal services such as incubators, technology transfer, research centers, and other collaborative opportunities. Though more scarce, there are also vibrant entrepreneurial university ecosystems. These universities are embedded within entrepreneurial regions and, through a lengthy process, develop the elements necessary to build an ecosystem and take on the many roles that help entrench it within the regional ecosystem.[109]

Because universities provide so much support to an entrepreneurial ecosystem, the towns and cities in which they are located also benefit. In terms of college towns that foster entrepreneurialism, Stanford is a role model. In fact, one of the reasons Silicon Valley became synonymous with technology and entrepreneurship was due to the influence of a Stanford University dean and provost. Dr. Frederick Terman built Stanford's engineering department by engaging in research for the government.[110] Known for taking advantage of opportunities, he created an industrial park on unused university land and encouraged two of his students, Bill Hewlett and David Packard, to form their own company there. Walt Disney was their first client.[111]

Stanford may have been the first entrepreneurial college town, but many peers have emerged over the years. The ecosystems in Ann Arbor, Boulder, and Denver exist partially due to the innovation found at their local universities. Ohio has Ohio State, University of Cincinnati, Xavier, and Miami of Ohio. Indiana is home to Purdue, Notre Dame, Butler, DePauw, and Indiana University. The clusters of universities in these and other cities create a pool of incredible talent that proliferates through the town, state, and country. The reputation of these schools and their impressive alumni lists continues to draw talent inward from the coasts and bolster the thriving entrepreneurial spirit of the flyover states.[112]

The two strongest entrepreneurial ecosystems in Arkansas are anchored by their respective local universities. Fayetteville, home of Startup Junkie and the University of Arkansas, collaborates with the Sam M. Walton College of Business and the McMillion Innovation Studio, a collaborative space designed for interdisciplinary groups to create and innovate together. This one-of-a-kind innovation hub was launched by a gift from Walmart CEO Doug McMillon and his wife Shelley to increase startup activity on the university campus, and it serves as another great example of the entrepreneurial legacy left to Northwest Arkansas by Walmart's founder Sam Walton.[113] In Conway, where the Conductor team is located, the University of Central Arkansas has a Makerspace that is open to students, faculty, and the public. Completely free for anyone to utilize, the UCA Makerspace helps entrepreneurs with prototyping, patent assistance, and equipment training.[114]

How can an ecosystem encourage entrepreneurial talent development in the local youth?

Though universities can be valuable assets in growing an entrepreneurial ecosystem, communities can begin fostering creativity and engineering skills long before students are of college age. The natural curiosity of children can provide enough out-of-the-box thinking to completely change an industry. Gabby Goodwin was seven years old when she developed a unique double sided hair clip and founded her company "Gabby's Bows."[115] Her journey has been documented in a children's book called *Gabby Invents the Perfect Hairbow* and tells of how an everyday frustration prompted the creation of a hair clip that is now worn by thousands of little girls. Sofia Overton was 11 years old when she participated in a Conductor event to pitch her Wise Pocket socks. Invented with a pocket to snuggly hold a cell phone, Sofia took her product to the national stage when she pitched it to the investors on Shark Tank.[116] There is no minimum age to become an entrepreneur, but the ecosystem must have the resources available to nurture young talent and connect them with tools that can help bring their business ideas to life.

An easy way for an ecosystem builder to foster young talent is to support art and creativity in the local classrooms. Research shows that children who show more imagination are better divergent thinkers and have higher creative thinking ability.[117] Simply being exposed to art and cultural institutions has tremendous benefits. Studies show that students who are exposed to museums and performing arts centers demonstrate significant and measurable differences in displaying tolerance, empathy, educational memory, and critical thinking skills.[118]

Accomplished entrepreneurs have begun to recognize the need to support youth entrepreneurial activities and are providing opportunities for ecosystems to develop young talent. Steve Case, former head of AOL and current Chair and CEO of Revolution, and Carly Fiorina, former Chair and CEO of Hewlett-Packard, proposed a national K-12 entrepreneurship challenge to expose young people to entrepreneurial thinking styles with particular attention to underserved children. Dozens of programs like this continue to be developed as extracurricular activities and also as an addition to classroom curriculum. In Austin, a high school and its feeder elementary and middle schools began an entrepreneurship program that culminates in a junior-year incubator. Students compete in the style of Shark Tank for grants from a local venture capital firm, and in their senior year they participate in an accelerator that runs the business.[119]

An ecosystem builder does not need connections in the school district or even contacts in the local university system to foster entrepreneurial talent. Talent is developed in communities by providing creative outlets, opportunities to practice complex problem solving skills, and access to research tools. Even if these activities take place in a county library, it could be a spark of innovation the ecosystem has been waiting for to ignite a blaze of local entrepreneurship.

How do entrepreneurs develop talent within their businesses?

The first step to strengthening the ecosystem talent pillar is growing entrepreneurs. The second step is growing the talent that entrepreneurs need for their ventures to be successful. An entrepreneur's strategy to hire, retain, and develop a superior workforce is commonly referred to as talent development. It is most successful when the entrepreneur or a manager (rather than a human resources representative or hiring firm) takes the lead in the recruitment and development process.[120] This approach also helps leaders and their employees build a relationship, which can lead to a more engaged team and reduced turnover in the company.[121]

A solid talent development plan should include clear vision, values, and goals to support the entrepreneur's objectives. One option is to complete a talent assessment of the company to identify any gaps in competencies or skills areas and to ensure there are diverse hiring practices from the very early stages of the startup. Talent development and assessment can occur through informal means like surveys or conversations or in official classes or workshops. The following items are some simple strategies for an entrepreneur to nurture their talented workforce.[122]

» Provide mentorship and coaching
» Offer regular assessments
» Debrief after projects
» Empower employee decision-making
» Cross-train across business units
» Create networking opportunities
» Earmark funding
» Lead by example

Ecosystem builders can help their local entrepreneurs grow talent by connecting them to experienced mentors who can help young entrepreneurs develop much-needed self-confidence. Studies consistently demonstrate that having a mentor is instrumental to success in business. While only about half of small businesses survive past five years, 70% of businesses that have been mentored survive longer.[123] Many entrepreneurs also start their companies on their own without any employees. As entrepreneurs begin to look for talent in the ecosystem, ecosystem builders can connect them to a larger network within the community and industry so they can find the best people for the job.[124] Talent development is a continuous process that includes exposing young people in the community to entrepreneurial-thinking strategies, leveraging local university and educational resources to create entrepreneurs, and assisting entrepreneurs in their own quest to find and sustain a talented workforce. An ecosystem that attracts, develops, and retains robust talent is a place that can plant, incubate, and grow strong small businesses.

CHAPTER 5:

Culture

How can an ecosystem foster an entrepreneurial culture? [125]

The second pillar to support a strong venture ecosystem is culture. For an ecosystem to successfully grow and support entrepreneurs, it must have a culture of innovation, collaboration, risk taking, and curiosity. Starting a business is challenging in and of itself, and without an ecosystem to provide an experienced pool of talent, existing infrastructure of other businesses, networks, support services, and funding, the likelihood of failure increases. For entrepreneurs to succeed, their community must support them. In addition to knowledge and capital, the community culture should demonstrate fortitude and recognize that failure and success go hand-in-hand. To promote networking and help navigate policy, entrepreneurs need strong connections and teams at local, regional, state, and federal levels.

Ecosystem builders can help by creating opportunities to increase entrepreneurs' visibility and connecting them with other entrepreneurs in the community. One way to do this is to identify resources and create a central portal for one-stop information shopping. Another key means of facilitating this connectivity is by ensuring a regular cadence of engaging events, programs, and activities that reinforce the entrepreneurial drum beat. The venture scene must be event-driven. The Startup Junkie and Conductor teams run over 200 events each year in Arkansas. These events lead to "creative collisions" and unexpected connections that strengthen the venture ecosystem and reinforce the support for entrepreneurialism within the "coalition of the willing" (entrepreneurs, investors, university people, community leaders, and others). When successful, this sort of event-driven approach combats one of entrepreneurs' greatest issues - feeling that they are all alone in their journey.

Another vital aspect of supporting an entrepreneurial culture is to embrace and celebrate change. The most successful entrepreneurial cities have embraced change and willingly adapted to new circumstances. Cities with an entrepreneurial attitude view change as an opportunity and welcome the challenges that go with it. They know that business and economic growth benefits the greater good through more spending on education and health initiatives, and they actively participate in efforts to ensure that happens.

What does an entrepreneurial culture look like?

One of the best ways to encourage an entrepreneurial culture is to help community leaders nurture entrepreneurialism in their established organizations. If City Hall, the school district, hospital systems, and grocery stores embrace entrepreneurialism internally, the result will be an overflow of innovative and creative citizens who welcome change and new ideas in the ecosystem. The culture of an organization encompasses the values, beliefs, and behaviors that contribute to its unique social and psychological environment.[126] Entrepreneurs are persistent, passionate, creative, motivated, resourceful, and risk-takers, and these characteristics become embedded in the culture of their organizations.[127]

An entrepreneurial culture in an organization provides a completely different experience for customers or clients. For example, consider two bike shops that take very different approaches to how they assist customers. The first may focus on helping customers reach their peak performance by observing them ride a fixed bike or analyzing a race video and going over each component to see where precious seconds might be cut from their time. As an entrepreneurial organization, this shop prioritizes the customer experience and wants to help customers solve their problems. The second bike shop may just try to sell bikes by having an unengaged part-time worker sitting behind a counter, possibly ignoring people as they walk in and allowing the customer to wander aimlessly around the shop without offering even a simple "hello."

Walking into either of these bike shops would immediately give a customer an idea of the culture that each leader fosters. Physical representations, or artifacts, are the first clue. The employees in the first store wear uniform polo shirts while those in the other store wear t-shirts and shorts. Each store has its own logo and speaks in the language of that store. A salesperson in the first store would greet each customer by saying, "Good afternoon, Sir, how may I help you?" But the salesperson in the second might say nothing at all. Observing the way employees interact with each other gives insight into culture as well. Employees may work together and call on others for help, or they may work independently without support. The design and layout of the shop and the products they offer also provide insight into an organization's culture.

Behind the scenes there are more indicators. Some organizations tell new team members stories about its development and history or share the long-lasting impact of heroes or heroines that preceded them as part of the socialization process. Certain rules and rituals may be overtly stated while others are learned more subtly, such as a helpful "recommendation" that you park in a different spot or arrive to work a few minutes earlier.

Culture is a two-way process; that is, the organization imposes its culture on members while at the same time each member contributes to shaping the culture. Culture is reflected in values, beliefs, and assumptions that often become so ingrained in members' actions that they implement this behavior even when they are not at work. The culture of an entrepreneurial ecosystem is greatly influenced by the culture of the community's existing organizations and leaders.

What are some best practices in the development of an entrepreneurial culture?

The shaping of an organization's entrepreneurial culture is an intentional effort at every level. The nature of entrepreneurship suggests an open and dynamic culture. When the entrepreneurial mindset is encouraged in every business, industry, and organization of a local community, the innovative perspective will trickle out and influence the way local citizens view the community and make decisions. Here are some best practices for local organizations to develop an entrepreneurial culture to influence community change from the inside out.

Hire entrepreneurs:[128]

Research has shown that organizational leadership often looks for people with qualities similar to their own. Managers may have to widen their perspective and consider those with different skills and divergent thinking patterns to attract entrepreneurs. This makes good sense in an entrepreneurial environment because a leader wants a talented workforce with drive, passion, and vision as they take the company's product or service to levels not previously imagined.

Be a Learning Organization:[129]

Training sessions are useful in their own way, but a true entrepreneurial spirit comes from constant learning. This may occur in a class but is just as likely to take place from observations, discussions, failures, success, and a variety of other nontraditional methods. Learning organizations don't stop when they find a solution to a problem. Instead, they dig until they find the root cause and then solve that problem – in ten different ways! Harvard professor Chris Argyris calls this double-loop learning. That is, if the conference room is too hot, a learning organization wouldn't just open a window (single-loop learning). Instead, they take apart the thermostat — and maybe the radiator and furnace — to see why the room is too hot and start experimenting with solutions. Entrepreneurs have a double-loop culture.

Empower the team:[130]

A leader puts a lot of time and thought into hiring decisions, so they shouldn't second-guess themselves once the new talent is on board. Team members should be given responsibilities and decision-making authority as well as accountability. Collaboration should be encouraged and the team should know that everyone is a resource that contributes to the wealth of knowledge and experience of the organization.

Encourage sharing:[131]

Many organizations operate in silos, revealing only those aspects of their business unit necessary for a given project. Entrepreneurial culture is one of openness. Leaders should ask for recommendations and show the team that they are valued. Leaders should be candid that they don't know everything and that they value their team's wisdom. All team members should be comfortable generating ideas and having the voice to share them. It should be clear that failures and successes both contribute to the mission, and either outcome can lead to the next great innovation.

Prioritize diversity:[132]

The need for diverse teams has been a much-discussed topic in the last decade, but its importance cannot be overstated. Diversity can refer to inherent traits (what one is born with) as well as acquired characteristics (experience and perspective). Companies that encourage diversity contribute to a culture of innovation by providing an environment where different opinions are valued and employees have a high tolerance for risk. And diversity isn't just a popular social notion: diverse organizations report 35% higher revenue than their homogenous counterparts.

How can an entrepreneurial culture be created naturally?

It is an ecosystem builder's responsibility to keep entrepreneurs front and center when developing community support. When an entrepreneur is the primary focus of the ecosystem, the culture will begin to organically shift from a traditional economic development approach to one more open to innovation and change. For the startup founder, the most rewarding feeling is to know that an idea they have been nurturing will come to fruition. For many entrepreneurs this reality transpires thanks to the generosity of funders, academic partners, or other entrepreneurial support organizations that are found in the ecosystem.

One connection that an ecosystem builder can help foster is between an entrepreneur and angel investors and venture capitalists. These funders support projects and people that they believe in and feel a connection with. An ecosystem builder should help to identify areas of commonality between the funding network and entrepreneurs and then provide opportunities for collision through events and activities. Entrepreneurs shouldn't shy away from asking questions to ensure their goals and growth plan are in sync. Ecosystem builders can help entrepreneurs do their homework and come to the table with a clear and well-defined plan. By having a clear vision and being able to communicate that vision to a funder, it is likely that founders and investors can work together to achieve a mutually rewarding experience.

Many communities in the flyover states do not have an active angel investor network, or the majority of the businesses in the community are not appropriate for venture capital. However, these entrepreneurs still need some source of funding to support their ventures. An ecosystem builder can be a resource for these business owners by organizing events that connect businesses to local bankers or microlenders, or by helping them to refine their business plan. It is still important for lifestyle entrepreneurs to develop and communicate a clear vision when seeking financial support. By assisting entrepreneurs at every stage, and keeping them front and center when designing community events and activities, an entrepreneurial culture will begin to flourish naturally as it moves throughout the ecosystem.

CHAPTER 6:

Community Engagement

What is community engagement?

The third pillar in entrepreneurial ecosystem building is community engagement. While creating entrepreneurial culture entails cultivating an attitude of innovation and curiosity, community engagement sparks the actions that result from that culture. In the context of an ecosystem, engagement is the interaction between entrepreneurs or other employers, employees, and other members of the community that results in measurable improvement in desired outcomes for all parties. Engagement can be seen at all levels, be it an advisor providing recommendations to an entrepreneur or two entities coming together to form a partnership.[133]

Community engagement is the collaborative efforts of groups of people related by geography, circumstance, or special interest to address their collective well-being. It involves partnerships and coalitions that can mobilize resources, influence systems and relationships, and serve as a catalyst for change. Pennsylvania State University's Center for Economic and Community Development describes community engagement as a blend of science and art. The science is reflected in the many disciplines that contribute to the literature and conceptual development, including sociology, public policy, organizational development, psychology, and anthropology. The art is reflected in the understanding and sensitivity necessary to apply the science to the unique needs of each community and their specific engagement efforts.[134]

Community engagement between entrepreneurs and civic and philanthropic groups can be done in many different ways. Examples include companies that participate in a day of service in their community, perhaps "adopting" a school or nonprofit and providing repair and clean-up services. Some organizations allow employees to donate an allotted amount of their work hours to individually volunteer with a nonprofit of their choosing. Businesses also provide support through donations to targeted initiatives and sponsorships of teams or events within their community. These individual and collective approaches build relationships and networks and contribute to developing a positive community culture regarding entrepreneurship. Employees pass on their skills and learn new skills in the process. These are great opportunities to experience teamwork in a different way. Morale is boosted and pride in the company and community is reinforced,[135] making it a win-win situation.

Community engagement is also demonstrated in the principal roles academic institutions play in entrepreneurial ecosystems. They take on the role of entrepreneurs by providing a creative environment for student and faculty innovation and extend that role through collaborations with businesses and government agencies. Increasingly, institutions are formalizing their commitment by offering degrees in entrepreneurship that offer courses in which students learn to develop networks, raise funding, and bring their ideas to market. Because learning entrepreneurialism and being an entrepreneur are two different things, these programs also typically provide opportunities for students to become involved in real-world entrepreneurial ventures.

Why is it important that a community, established companies, and institutions all engage in the entrepreneurial ecosystem?

We have discussed the importance of a strong entrepreneurial ecosystem in attracting entrepreneurs and how this has a positive ripple effect throughout that system and community. Engagement from the community, businesses, and institutions adds another dimension to the ecosystem. It allows individuals and other voices outside of the immediate process to have a meaningful role in the projects and programs that will impact them and their communities.

Within the entrepreneurial ecosystem, engagement brings forth more ideas and opportunities. It gathers together people from different facets of the population who might not have the chance to interact if not for a common entrepreneurial interest. This broadens the network of the entrepreneur and generates the possibility of alliances among others in the network. For example, volunteers from a tech company who provide lessons on coding to high school students might meet up with a parent who is trying to create a competition. The volunteers go back and encourage their boss to sponsor the event. Professors from the university are brought in as judges and talk up their institutions to the finalists during the break. Connections are made, businesses are strengthened, new students are registered, and goals are achieved.

When someone stands in as an agent for their organization, there is an assumption that the individual is the messenger bringing forth the unanimous view of their members. This might be a councilperson, corporate public relations representative, or university dean or president. While it is likely true that this agent represents the opinion of their own organization, it would be short-sighted to assume that these individuals fully represent their greater communities. University presidents likely share similar concerns compared to the corporate leader, but the small private liberal arts college may have very different funding priorities than the large state-funded public research university across town. Similarly, the stockbroker parents of students who push for a later start to the school day may not be considering the childcare needs of single parents who work two jobs with very little flexibility in their schedules. An entrepreneurial ecosystem builder should try to walk a mile in everyone's shoes to better understand each community member's perspective and concerns.

Creating opportunities for engagement evens the playing field. Individuals and groups who may otherwise be underrepresented are given equal footing with those who have greater wealth or position. Every concern may not be resolved, but through engagement, awareness is sparked, ideas are developed, and programs are introduced. A diversity of voices creates inclusion, a sense of ownership, and commitment to ideas.

How can an ecosystem builder drive engagement across the various constituencies?

Communities with ecosystem builders have a head start when it comes to driving opportunities for engagement. Ecosystem builders take a long-term, system-wide approach to fostering innovation and entrepreneurship in their communities. They are systems-thinkers and draw on that approach to connect the resources needed to build a thriving ecosystem. These people or groups increase the ecosystem's well-being and impact by constantly networking, finding and matchmaking new members, managing relationships, and spreading the word about ecosystem activity.[136]

The Startup Champions Network (SCN) is a great example of ecosystem building. Entrepreneurial themselves, the members of SCN work across the nation to support entrepreneurs by developing diverse communities, increasing their access to resources, and providing professional development. It is community-driven in that it supports the individuals that support entrepreneurship in their area. Where others might see barriers, they see possibilities and promote the mantra "Give Before Your Get." Perhaps most importantly, they also track a common set of metrics to monitor the health of the ecosystem, which acts as a benchmark for local regions and a report card of the strength of the national ecosystem.[137]

Because ecosystems include a diverse range of roles, ecosystem builders are critical to bringing disparate pieces of the puzzle together. The research university might be well-known for incubating innovation, but the smaller school may have a strong social justice or software development program that would provide critical links within the ecosystem. Likewise, everyone in a city might be able to see the logo of its biggest corporation in the skyline but may be unaware that the small businesses surrounding it keep it running efficiently. Ecosystem builders know about the big school and the small school, the major corporation and the mom-and-pops. And then they make sure everyone else in the system knows about them too.

The Kauffman Foundation is leading the charge to formalize the field of ecosystem building on a global scale. They refer to this work as the ESHIP initiative, and they have created a wide variety of ecosystem building resources, including the Ecosystem Building Playbook, to outline the need for ecosystem builders to unite to support entrepreneurship.[138] Using a mass collaboration approach, 400+ ecosystem builders convened in Kansas City to create the Seven ESHIP Goals, each with a specific objective of growing and strengthening the field and promoting entrepreneurship as the most important form of economic development.[139]

What are some best practices for community engagement in the ecosystem? [140]

As with any new initiative, it is important to have clear goals to achieve the highest level of engagement. Here are some best practices to help plan and design effective community engagement.

Identify relevant stakeholders:

Be comprehensive and inclusive in recognizing local interest groups. Make a concerted effort to contact any underrepresented religious, cultural, racial, and ethnic groups. Also, out of sight should not be out of mind — don't forget virtual and web-based groups.

Build trust:

While working with many different constituents, it is important to be respectful of people's time, knowledge, and experience. Forming relationships and building inroads with communities will go a long way when trying to get an event or initiative off the ground. When people's businesses or ideas are on the line, there will be no innovation or knowledge shared without trust, so ecosystem builders have to refrain from assumptions and judgment and remain open minded and honest.

Remove barriers to engagement:

Consider where and how you will communicate. Accessibility to meetings or other gatherings by public transportation is important; so, too, is recognition that not everyone will have or be comfortable providing identification to enter a building. Provide materials or accommodations for different languages and physical abilities and give consideration to different levels of literacy; this includes use of jargon, technical language, and acronyms. And don't forget the single parents with two jobs who may have their children with them – have childcare and, if appropriate, snacks available.

Offer different formats for engagement:

Town halls and other public meetings are a great way to reach a large group of people at once, but they can become unruly and ineffective if the issue is controversial or a heated debate arises. Breaking out into smaller groups following the initial overview is more intimate and allows for greater discussion. Focus groups and workshops are also a great way to exchange information and gather input on issues. Smaller groups also allow opportunities to address language or other possible barriers to participation. Virtual opportunities can increase participation by allowing participants to engage at a time and location convenient to their schedule.

Don't discount opportunities for engagement that occur outside of formal gatherings. A community event is an ideal time to speak with people individually or in small groups where they feel more comfortable connecting. Hosting a social event such as lunch with a councilperson or game night at a recreation center are other options. Each table should include a community representative who can raise issues and facilitate discussions.

Establish ground-rules:

Let participants know everyone's roles and the goals for the interaction. Identify any non-negotiable topics; this may include maintaining sponsor anonymity or withholding data outcomes before analysis is complete. Be sure to identify time limits for those who are more long-winded and establish a culturally-shared norm for those who may be more reticent to speak.

Do the right thing:

When you bring people together to engage them, let them engage. Listen more than you speak and put yourself in their position to better understand their perspective. Be transparent about what can and can not be achieved. Never bring people together under the pretense of being interested in their stories if you have no intention of incorporating their experiences. This defies the goals of the ecosystem and negates any gains already achieved.

Community engagement is the thread that weaves together the components of the ecosystem and helps secure the four pillars in place. Entrepreneurs need the community to support their ventures, and communities need small businesses to create vibrant places to live, work, and play.

CHAPTER 7:

Capital

How does capital fuel the development of an ecosystem?

The fourth pillar of a strong venture ecosystem is the availability and accessibility of financial capital. As we established in Chapter 5, an entrepreneurial culture must be led by entrepreneurs. In order for founders to start and grow their companies, they must be able to identify and secure the type of capital that is best for them. An ecosystem builder's role is to connect a business owner with the type of capital they need, whether through a traditional bank loan or a venture-backed investment. An exciting part of this process is often helping an entrepreneur recognize a technological or business gap and providing them with the information needed to fill that gap. The most frustrating - or infuriating - outcome of this process is if an entrepreneur has to walk away from pursuing an opportunity and possibly influencing a long-term impact because they lack funding. While people and relationships are the foundation of successful businesses and ecosystems, it takes cold, hard cash to get them up and running. Not surprisingly, finding talent and startup capital are among the biggest challenges entrepreneurs face.

Victor Hwang, former President of Entrepreneurship at the Kauffman Foundation, is convinced that thousands of potentially world-changing innovations fail each year because they are unable to secure capital. He also notes that a "free market" where capital flows efficiently is generally true in name only.[141] For example, Silicon Valley accounts for almost 45% of total capital venture investments in the U.S.,[142] leaving the vast majority of the country trying to access just about the same amount of funding as a fifty-square mile dot on the map in northern California.

Why is access to capital important for business health?

As with all businesses, funding keeps the fires burning bright – perhaps literally! To start, entrepreneurs need seed money to buy equipment, find a workspace, start a website, print business cards, and everything else needed to get the business started. Some people rely on their own savings or ask close family and friends for this initial funding. For many, however, outside investors are the best way to find funding, and this typically requires giving up part of the equity. [143]

Once a business is established and functioning, a steady cash flow is essential to keep the business operational. Utility costs, insurance, health care, taxes, salaries, and a host of other expenses must be paid. One burning question for entrepreneurs is whether or not they should pay themselves. There are different schools of thought on this. One approach is for them to view themselves as an employee or consultant, estimate their hourly value, and include that amount in their business plan. Another view is to opt for a more modest salary, taking just what is needed to get by. Once the business becomes profitable, they can reevaluate to see if it makes sense for them to get a raise. Some business owners might tie a salary increase to company growth; that is, if their business grows 20%, they take a 20% increase. It may seem counterintuitive to take money from the business they are working so hard to build, but an entrepreneur wouldn't ask someone else to work for free and as such they shouldn't put that burden on themselves.[144] [145] An ecosystem builder can help by sitting with an entrepreneur and walking them through the options or connecting them with a local expert who can help address all their questions.

Entrepreneurs also need to give consideration to unexpected costs. A vehicle involved in an accident, customer refunds for lost or damaged shipments, or a flood in the basement could require a substantial outlay of costs. There will also be maintenance and upgrades to phones, computers, and software. If an entrepreneur has all of this covered and then some, they may be in a position to expand their business. While any costs associated with expanding a business should be offset by the increase in revenue, there may be a gap between when expenditures occur and when business growth is achieved. These types of scenarios must be considered in advance to avoid falling behind before you get started.

Achieving business goals requires funding, and a strong ecosystem provides these opportunities. Before approaching a potential funder, it is important that the founder has a realistic valuation of the startup. Venture capital firms will want equity in the business, and a founder will need to determine how much he or she is willing to give up. Developing a strong business plan will help a business owner determine the worth of a startup three to five years out. Investors will appreciate the accurate representation, and it also helps guide the entrepreneur in knowing how much money to raise. While more may seem better, raising too much money won't produce a good return on investment.[146]

It's worth noting again the relationship aspect of entrepreneurship. Funders are clearly a critical part of an entrepreneur's success, but entrepreneurs should do their homework on venture capitalists and other possible funders to find a good fit. Top venture capital firms, which are very competitive, are often led by partners who themselves have been entrepreneurs as opposed to lower-tier firms, which are led by bankers.[147] This is an important distinction because venture capitalists manage assets and bankers manage money. Longtime entrepreneur, venture capitalist and entrepreneurial advocate Victor Hwang agrees, noting that a commonality among great venture capitalists is that they are empathetic and in sync with the entrepreneur and passionate about their business. They understand what the entrepreneur is going through and will help them work through the process. He also notes that venture capitalists should be loyal to the ecosystem, generating value to the community rather than focusing on their return from a single deal.[148] An ecosystem builder can help connect the entrepreneur to the source of capital that is best for them.

What is an angel investor?

When an ecosystem has high quality talent, an innovative culture of entrepreneurial thinking, and robust community engagement, people begin to notice. One important source of capital that an entrepreneur should aim to appeal to is an angel investor. Angel investors are high net-worth people who provide financing for new startups or business expansion.[149] Most angels are designated as "accredited" by the Securities and Exchange Commission, meaning they have at least $1 million in assets and a minimum income of $200,000; however, this is not a requirement for investing.[150] Although angel investors are not in the same category as venture capital firms, they are unambiguously wealthy and well-equipped to provide more than adequate seed money or other startup costs.[151] It is in any ecosystem builder's best interest to seek out potential angel investors and create events and activities to introduce them to budding startups.

Angel investing is a unique league of its own. There are no defined limits in terms of the amount of an angel investment. A typical investment might fall between $10,000 to $100,000, but $500,000 is not out of the question.[152] Some investors may offer a loan, but most seek equity of 25% or more.[153] While angel investors are always on the lookout for new and interesting opportunities, they recognize the risk involved and, accordingly, reject about 75% of proposals.[154]

Like venture capitalists, angel investors are meticulous in reviewing potential applicants. They look for a solid business plan with the potential of a high return on investment - 20 to 40 percent.[155] They also look closely at the qualifications of the management team. Frequently, angels are or have been entrepreneurs themselves and may want to be actively involved in the endeavor and have a seat on the Board of Directors.[156] Angel investors often go with their gut feeling and rely on their perception of the entrepreneur. A flawed business model by someone the investor feels a positive connection to is more likely to be funded than a stronger model from someone the investor does not connect with. This is another reason why ecosystem builders should cultivate opportunities for relationship building between entrepreneurs and potential funding sources.[157]

Increasingly, a group or syndicate of accredited angels will create an investing network. Individual angels contribute to the syndicate, and a professional management team identifies investments of interest to that group. An individual angel can be a member of more than one syndicate to create a more diversified portfolio.[158] Being part of a syndicate allows angels to work with like-minded investors while sharing the risks and benefits of investing. Some advantages of being part of an angel syndicate are the pooling of financial resources, experience, and networks coming together for a common purpose. An established syndicate benefits from recognition at a greater level than its individual members would receive. Working within an ecosystem provides great opportunities to create angel networks because investors are more likely to support companies in their communities. Local attorneys, accountants, or Chambers of Commerce can help direct you to possible syndicates.[159]

What are the best practices of angel network management?

The Ark Angel Alliance is a group managed by the Conductor that connects early stage companies with angels in the participating network. Part of effective management includes keeping transparency as the core principle in any angel investment forum. Policies and metrics for what the group will or will not invest in, membership criteria, and expenses are just some of the issues that should be determined before investing in any deal. Also, all members should bear an equal burden in terms of investment – everyone writes a check at the same time and for the same amount.[160]

Angel syndicates and their managers should make it easy for the entrepreneur. They should offer one point of contact and invest as an LLC rather than individual investors. The angel network should be specific in how it can support the entrepreneur with their experience and contacts to further ensure success.[161]

Conducting rigorous due diligence mitigates risk to investors. Gaining a comprehensive understanding of the entrepreneur and his or her business allows for a better determination of suitability within the syndicate's portfolio.[162] Members should take an active role in the group and work with their management team in screening potential investments. A thriving ecosystem includes not only access to funds, but also people to help access it. Research shows that advisors are critical resources and add substantial value, especially when entrepreneurs have limited experience dealing with venture capitalists.[163]

What is the funding continuum?

The financial growth cycle for early-stage ventures is what we refer to as the funding continuum. Businesses are funded based on their size, age, and what is known about them. Early-stage ventures are often initially funded by the entrepreneur. The entrepreneur might seek support from partners, friends, and family (sometimes referred to as the "FFF" round: friends, family, and fools!). To get the business beyond concept and early sales, further financing is sometimes sought from angels and venture capitalists. Eventually, later stage growth equity and private equity might be an option for growth or as a set up for an acquisition exit.

Though equity-based crowdfunding was legalized with the 2012 Jobs Act, the enabling regulations are nearly as rigorous as a regular public offering. As a result, equity-based crowdfunding hasn't grown to be a widely used alternative means of finance. The same fate could be projected for initial coin offerings (ICOs) as scalable ventures that contemplated ICOs have been deterred from exploring this possibility since the Securities and Exchange Commission has placed the process under significant scrutiny.

All stages of other funding options become available such as CDFIs, Kiva, and other peer-to-peer lending solutions. For example, commercial lending is an option for scaling a business if it has enough liquidation, and if an initial public offering is in the works, hedge funds may show an interest. Companies that go public can issue corporate debt.[164]

The funding continuum (from angel through private equity) is definitely needed, but more often than not, the capital markets are ruthlessly efficient. Many ventures that don't receive funding shouldn't receive funding because the founders are not a solid bet, don't have a shot at scaling, and couldn't create a sustainable competitive advantage. In addition, the fixation with raising capital rewards the wrong behaviors. Make no mistake: less than one percent (1%) of all ventures will ever raise venture capital. The rest of the startup and small business scene succeeds by sticking to the fundamentals of solving a problem a customer will pay for and delivering value.

Consider the outcome Nick Dozier enjoyed when he built Atlas Technologies (a data visualization company that had Walmart and other large enterprises as customers) and took no outside capital versus Ryan Frazier, who built DataRank (a social listening platform), which took capital from YC, 500 Startups, and several angels and VC firms. When Atlas was sold to Advantage for an undisclosed amount, Nick owned 100 percent of the company. He did so well in this deal that he had to create a substantial family office to manage the proceeds. Ryan and his co-founders sold DataRank to Simply Measured for a no-cash stock swap. Simply Measured then rode the combined business into the ground despite having capital and oversight from a top tier Silicon Valley VC. A venture ecosystem builder with solid business acumen and knowledge of investment options can help the entrepreneur determine the pros and cons of the different funding opportunities and make the best decision about which route to pursue.

What should entrepreneurs do after raising capital?[165]

Raising capital is hard work and it is natural for entrepreneurs to want to celebrate such a milestone. Most investors agree that going through the funding process is arduous and taking a moment to acknowledge that makes sense. However, the end goal is not to only raise money: it is to create and run a viable company. Ecosystem builders can help entrepreneurs celebrate their successes but also keep them on track to realize their full entrepreneurial dreams.

First, it is important to recognize a team that has put in great effort to advance their business. Breaking out a few beers or a bottle of bubbly and extending gratitude for hard work and a shout-out to key players helps build morale and momentum. It also validates the extensive effort required to get funding and recognizes that it's a team effort. But if, at this stage, the celebration moves from the office to the ballroom, a reality check could be in order for the startup.

One view is that anything beyond a quick high-five sends the wrong message to the ecosystem. Sure, receiving funding is important, but that's part of an entrepreneur's job. One school of thought suggests that receiving funding should not be viewed as a milestone but as a stepping stone on the entrepreneurial path. Thanks and appreciation are always appropriate and should be distributed generously. Raising capital is important, but not nearly as important as driving product or service sales. Celebrations have their place, but an entrepreneur should focus on creating a positive and supportive work environment as a more sustainable long-term approach for recognizing the effort and contributions of the company's talent. Also, if funding doesn't come through, it is not necessarily a reflection of the team's effort or lack thereof. In the spirit of perpetuating an entrepreneurial culture, it is appropriate to celebrate the failure as well.

What are key strategies to avoid investor fatigue?

When investors are losing money or not making as much as they anticipated, they experience what we refer to as "investor fatigue."[166] While emerging venture ecosystems are growing the pipeline of startups that have a chance to scale, it can take years or even decades to build to the point that there are frequent exits, and investor returns are even a possibility. If the pipeline of startups is largely comprised of IP-intensive and/or life sciences ventures, the possibility of a regular cadence of exits is even less likely. When this happens, investors can become stressed or anxious, which affects their decisions. To avoid the potential negative outcomes associated with being too reactive, it is important for an ecosystem builder to learn to manage investment fatigue.

A perfect example of this reality can be seen through the experience of VIC Technology Venture Development in Arkansas. This firm has been in place for more than fifteen years incubating and growing IP-intensive startups based on university IP. The total portfolio is more than fifteen ventures. Though several are very promising, there has only been one positive exist to date. BlueInGreen, a VIC portfolio water quality venture recently sold to an acquiring firm in Georgia. The portfolio companies have largely been funded by SBIR/STTR grants, angel investments, and a few strategic corporate investments. Even with the difficulties and lack of exits thus far, VIC Technology Venture Development serves a crucial function in commercializing promising university IP. The key to their ongoing success and survival will be finding very patient investors and growing the overall size of the portfolio to increase the probability of more frequent exits. The VIC experience is not unique - other venture ecosystems in flyover states that have a large number of life sciences ventures tied to university IP face similar realities.

Setting expectations about the frequency of exits is very important. Realistically, early-stage investing will involve lots of early venture failures. Exits, when they do occur, will be 7-15 years after the initial investment. As an asset class, this lack of immediate gratification and liquidity can lead to investor fatigue and a loss of interest. To address the long-term nature of exits, early-stage fund managers should consider including venture debt or revenue-based royalty finance as a potential deal structure. These sorts of structures can provide more regular returns to investors for at least a portion of the portfolio.

What are some other sources of capital in an ecosystem?

Capital comes in many forms and it is important for ecosystem builders to know generally how each affects a business. Non-dilutive sources of finance do not require that the entrepreneur give away any equity in the business. This includes debt capital. The most typical type of non-dilutive debt funding is a loan. Debt capital must be repaid with interest at regular intervals over a defined period. This means that once a business owner has finished paying back the debt, their liability is over. In some cases, taking on debt offers tax deductions. Whether or not this is the case, debt financing keeps full ownership of the business with the entrepreneur.

The big risk of taking on debt is that the borrower must repay it regularly regardless of how successful (or unsuccessful) the business is. If a business takes on too much debt or misses payments, the valuation of the business can be affected. This might limit or prevent the opportunity for raising additional capital. Financing terms can also change if the debt has a variable interest rate or balloon payment.[167]

Licensing a project to a partner in the industry is another non-dilutive way to create revenue. Some businesses are eligible for tax credits, though these monies would be refunded after expenses are incurred. Using a royalty financing model, a group of investors provides capital in exchange for a percentage of future revenues. Grants also fall under this category, though these are generally limited to projects with an academic connection.[168]

Alternatively, an equity financing agreement requires that the entrepreneur give away partial ownership of his or her business in exchange for capital. This amount typically starts in the range of 15-25% but increases with each round of funding, and it is possible that an investor may end up as an equal partner with half of the business.[169] Equity financing offers significantly more capital than debt and brings access to a wealth of experience through investors who want the business to succeed. Of course, this comes at the expense of ownership share.

With any type of funding, it is critical to be clear on terms and expectations from the outset. The amount of capital needed and stage of business are key factors in determining the best options. For example, non-dilutive funding allows entrepreneurs to retain equity, but they may need to pay ahead or pay back funds. If the funding need is so high that paying it back would be prohibitive, equity capital might be a better route. A thriving entrepreneurial community has the resources and the know-how to help entrepreneurs navigate the multitude of funding options.

How can entrepreneurs build scalable ventures without seeking capital?[170] [172]

To restate our mantra: entrepreneurial talent is key. Everyone on the business team has the ability to contribute or detract from the bottom line. When hiring, a business owner should make smart decisions and consider how each person can contribute to revenue, even if he or she is not in a direct revenue-producing role. An administrative person might have experience negotiating, and a tech person may have the ability to view the product from the customer's perspective to ensure a positive user experience. An ecosystem builder's network can also provide experienced insights from someone who has been in a similar situation or industry.

There are simple ways an entrepreneur can save cash and self-fund their venture. By remaining frugal, funds can be directed where they will have the greatest impact. Entrepreneurs can pack a peanut butter and jelly sandwich for their own lunch but take clients somewhere nice. Business owners can skip the nonessentials and invest in their product or service. Also, the barter system has lasted for centuries for a reason – an ecosystem builder can provide opportunities to entrepreneurs to trade their talent and skills. For example, conference volunteers typically attend for free. If an entrepreneur signs up for registration duty, they can attend the event and receive the added benefit of meeting the key players in their industry!

Entrepreneurs can be ready to launch without having a perfect product. Time is a commodity, and deciding whether an app should have three or five widgets is not worth the lost revenue of delaying its launch. Instead, founders can incorporate a feedback loop from customers, perhaps offering an incentive (a sixth widget?!) to encourage customers to respond. Entrepreneurs can also explore customer-funding options. Even with a discount, quarterly or annual prepayments for a product or service provides needed funding and added flexibility. The highest rate of growth for a startup occurs in the first two or three years,[173] so entrepreneurs can be creative in what they ask for and how they respond to requests. Through community engagement activities, entrepreneurs can connect with their local customer base to find the option that works best for them.

PART 3:

Leveraging Best Practices

CHAPTER 8:

Start Where You Are

The four pillars of ecosystem building consist of talent, culture, community engagement, and capital. Tapping into an existing infrastructure is one thing, but what if the community isn't quite there yet? Understanding and assessing the assets, aspirations, and community gaps is a crucial first step. Smaller cities and towns may live in the shadow of metropolitan areas, but they can still become an entrepreneurial hub by building on their own unique strengths and resources.

How does a community assess where they are?

For ecosystem builders to know where to start in evaluating their current community assets, they must take stock of what they can offer to support entrepreneurship and what they have yet to develop. One way to do this is to conduct a market analysis of the community.[174] This type of in-depth study identifies types and sizes of existing businesses, potential customers, and market needs. Although market analyses typically include a section on competitors, in the case of assessing a community for its ability to become a hub for entrepreneurs, the competitor analysis could be an extension of the business analysis. Knowing about local businesses provides insight about their volume, employees, services provided, support services, and other critical information. This helps identify strengths and gaps in a potential ecosystem. It also helps identify what level of entrepreneurship already exists.

An important part of a market analysis is to identify any barriers or obstacles to starting a business, including policies and regulations. Government regulations can make or break a welcoming community. An entrepreneur-friendly local government directly influences how businesses operate and they can work to encourage change at the regional or state level. For example, registering as a business and completing necessary forms and paperwork is a time-consuming effort. Local governments can simplify their regulations for starting a business and seek input from existing businesses to identify and eliminate confusing or superfluous steps. An online portal that includes necessary forms, contact information, FAQs, and other resources will streamline the process and let entrepreneurs know that the government is working toward their success, not detracting from it.

Many entrepreneurs start out working or distributing products from their home. Zoning codes should allow for the existence of combined business/residential properties. For businesses located outside the home, an inviting environment will draw both entrepreneurs and customers. Walkable business districts encourage residents and visitors to spend time in the downtown area. This creates greater tax revenue per square foot than other types of development. Local government and businesses can do their part by slowing traffic, adding benches, and beautifying the area.[174]

Policy and decision makers are also instrumental figures in local networks. These representatives should demonstrate their commitment to development in their community and region by working to attract not only entrepreneurs but other key elements of the infrastructure. If the area is home to a university, strong links and open lines of communication to the community should be facilitated. If not, encouraging a strong anchor business whose product and values are aligned with the region should be a priority. This high-level presence demonstrates mutual commitment from the business and community to support one another and the development of the region.

In addition to politicians, support from other key figures such as CEOs, lawyers, investors, and the local press can be used as an advantage. Sharing resources, hosting events, and providing coverage of the contributions of local start-ups gives a clear indication that entrepreneurial culture is (or will be) reflective of all facets of the community. Similarly, creating opportunities for entrepreneurs to share their stories, successes, and failures with others who have had similar experiences is a critical component of information-sharing that is core to entrepreneurial practice.[175]

Smaller communities and towns should not be deterred from encouraging entrepreneurship based on their size or location. Community leaders can reach out to local entrepreneurs and their own networks to identify needs and opportunities, and they can reach out to local businesses to build relationships and expand networks. The effort that communities invest is returned through the positive ripple-effect in the economy and region.

One resource that could be helpful to ecosystem builders looking to assess their community is the Venture Ecosystem Building Canvas found in the back of this book. A tool created by the Startup Junkie and Conductor teams, this comprehensive assessment aids in mapping community assets that support the four pillars of ecosystem building. With questions focused on Talent, Culture, Community Engagement, and Capital, the Canvas helps to identify readily available community resources and highlight areas of improvement to increase collaboration and entrepreneurial activities.

Why is starting with networking, programs, and events the right approach for most communities?

There is no shortage of opportunities to meet like-minded people in today's world. This opens the door to nearly unlimited resources for entrepreneurs and communities, whether starting from the ground up or filling in a few missing pieces along the way. For example, LinkedIn and Meetup are well-known platforms for a wide range of entrepreneurial groups. A recent search for different entrepreneurial groups yielded results for youth, women, and creative entrepreneurs, entrepreneurs focused on specific areas (including food and social entrepreneurship), and meetings in different cities and countries. There is something for everyone, and if the group doesn't exist, it's easy to create a new one.

Entrepreneurial programs and networking events provide opportunities to share ideas and best practices or to get help overcoming an obstacle a community might be facing. These groups offer professional and social networking, strategy and marketing insights, recruiting opportunities, and introduction to potential funders. You may find answers to questions you didn't even know you had!

Entrepreneurs can also find connections and opportunities through alumni organizations, social and religious organizations, and government programs. Additionally, there are any number of professional associations representing different industries, memberships, and causes that have local chapters throughout the country. These groups host professional and social events, and many offer speaking or award opportunities as a benefit of membership. Joining an online community offers the added advantages of bridging distance and the flexibility of non-synchronous activity.

In addition to joining a group or attending an event, communities can create workshops to encourage entrepreneurship. Business owners can offer a class on topics of interest to startups, such as accounting or marketing, or they can join forces with a university to host a conference on a range of topics. "Global Entrepreneur Week," "Startup Week," and "Small Business Saturday" are increasingly popular events that can be celebrated in any community; communities can build on this and other recognized events or create their own small, ecosystem-specific business recognition day. Incubators offer entrepreneurs a communal space to share ideas and challenges and benefit from mentors and advisors. Communities can collaborate with a university to start an incubator, or if resources are limited, they can arrange informal gatherings. A local business might offer a space and guidance, or a community room can be reserved for weekly meetings.

When searching for or joining a community, online or face-to-face, be sure to look at the other participants and the group's goals. You may come across a very active group of energetic, action-oriented members, but if their focus is identifying venture capital for biotech projects and your focus is building and home design, move on to something more in line with your community's needs. Likewise, a lot of activity can be a good thing, but you don't want to get lost in the shuffle. A good leader or facilitator makes a big difference in how a group interacts, so look around until you find a good fit.

It is equally important to be a good group member. Groups grow and benefit from the quality of their participants, so be prepared to bring something to the table beyond your own needs. Practice your 30-second introduction and have plenty of business cards. Give as much as you get—listen to others to see how you might be a resource and benefit from each other's knowledge.

Providing networking opportunities through various means is an excellent way for a community to support and build entrepreneurship. Doing so addresses all the pillars by contributing to the entrepreneurial culture and creating opportunities to engage with talent and other representatives of the community, including funders. Finally, since angel investors are often entrepreneurs themselves who like to support local projects, networking can lead to entrepreneurs funding other entrepreneurs.

How can you leverage your community's unique advantages?

Your community has its own unique strengths and assets. However, no matter how hard you try, you probably won't come to be known as the next Silicon Valley. While its example offers valuable lessons for new entrepreneurs, local communities should strive to be best at what they do best. Ecosystems that have succeeded have done so because they built on their existing expertise. This process can be simplified as a journey to understand a region's assets, aspirations, and market realities. Silicon Valley has become eponymous with technology because it identified and filled an unmet gap and did so brilliantly. If an ecosystem builder attaches "Silicon" as part of the title for a regional entrepreneurial initiative, it shows a fundamental lack of creativity and depth of thought about what will really differentiate a regional startup movement. Minnesota became the hub for food and agriculture.[177] The D.C. region has become the go-to location for biotech.[178] Northwest Arkansas is a leader in the supply chain.[179] These communities attracted entrepreneurs and top talent because they recognized and developed their own strengths rather than trying to duplicate or mirror another region's accomplishments.

Looking inward to identify regional strengths also compels communities to focus on their regional needs. Communities recognize what holds them back from being competitive or limits their ability to showcase their resources. The members of a community are its lifeblood and are aware of its imperfections and potential, and they are vested in creating opportunities for themselves, their children, and their neighbors. It is this intensive, intimate knowledge that distinguishes one community from another and it is these unique attributes that each community should leverage.

Harvard Business School Professor Josh Lerner's book, *Boulevard of Broken Dreams: Why Public Efforts to Boost Entrepreneurship and Venture Capital Have Failed -- and What to Do About It*, highlights the "foolish things" cities and states have done to try and create a startup ecosystem. Based on his extensive experience and observations, he recommends that government leaders examine local impediments to entrepreneurship and work with the private sector to develop a plan to address them. His colleague, Karen Gordon Mills, agrees. She proposes that local leaders analyze their assets to determine which are "world-class" and then create a competition to encourage the emergence of startups to build businesses around these assets.[180]

Does your ecosystem need help identifying world-class assets? Start by looking at the history of the region and the industries that contributed to its growth. This can help leaders understand their community's value. Yet it is also important to look beyond business contributions. Many of the emerging ecosystems are in cities known for their relaxed lifestyle and culture. Good schools, sustainability, parks and recreation, and arts contribute to a location's appeal. Don't forget that attributes like creativity, generosity, and patience are valued and should be promoted with other assets.

CHAPTER 9:

Programs & Events That Work

Entrepreneurial communities are growing across the country and throughout the flyover states. In fact, as these areas continue to develop and draw new entrepreneurs, they may lose their status as flyover states and instead become destinations.

Building an entrepreneurial ecosystem takes time, which is one reason why flyover states are increasingly popular. The people in the heartland of America are self-reliant and work hard to succeed in life. When there is a problem, they figure out a way to solve it themselves rather than wait for someone to come to their rescue. No wonder they are a beacon for entrepreneurs!

Still, there are those who try to create shortcuts. Some entrepreneurs, and many corporations who allege to promote entrepreneurialism, are engaged in high levels of activity that yield no apparent impact. Among entrepreneurs this is referred to as "Innovation Theater" — a lot of smoke and mirrors. But when the dust settles, there's just a person behind the curtain.

This can be seen in corporations that create accelerators or "Shark Tank" programs for the spectacle and drama of it all. They encourage employees to vie for funding for their innovative ideas but rarely provide resources to help these would-be entrepreneurs to identify customer needs or validate the existence of a problem. Without these metrics, the idea or presentation (or presenter) with the most flash and personality are typically rewarded rather than the innovation that best addresses an actual need.[181]

What are some best practices for programs and events from the flyover states?

Creating something from nothing can be daunting, and while every entrepreneur and ecosystem is unique, there are commonalities across systems that can provide benefits and offer a lasting impact. In this section we look at how different ecosystems have created programs and events that have helped them grow and develop their custom system.

Wisconsin – Moving Forward

Wisconsin remains in the low rankings based on Kauffman's Indicators of Entrepreneurship, but their presence is growing. In 2018, the number one company on Inc. magazine's list of the 5000 fastest-growing companies was a startup from Wisconsin; so was the seventh-ranked company.[181] Startup Wisconsin recently launched an initiative offering programming and networking events to develop and support emerging companies, including Startup Wisconsin Week, to celebrate entrepreneurship across the state. A look at their calendar shows multiple events every weekday in several of the twelve cities it supports. These events cover a range of issues under the umbrellas of networking, strategy, technology, sales and marketing, talent acquisition, diversity, and more.[182] Among their options are 1 Million Cups, a program started by the Kauffman Foundation to engage and inspire entrepreneurs that became instantly popular and is now used throughout the country.[183]

The Wisconsin Economic Development Corporation, a public-private partnership, also hosts events to promote statewide economic development. Their programs focus primarily on funding opportunities, including grants and seed funding through an accelerator, and they also have a Young Professionals Organization.[184] The Wisconsin Technology Council, an independent nonprofit that advises the Governor and Legislature, also hosts several conferences, symposia, summits, and business plan contests targeting students, entrepreneurs, companies, and investors.[185]

As with all successful ecosystems, universities play a key role in supporting entrepreneurship for their students and community. For the past six years the University of Wisconsin has hosted a "Wisconsin Entrepreneurship Showcase Event," with presentations from both in-state and out-of-state entrepreneurs as well as networking opportunities. The university also hosts a Distinguished Entrepreneurs Lunch program, where entrepreneurs advise and speak with undergraduate and graduate students at an Entrepreneur Training Program.[186]

Ohio – All Things are Possible

Ohio's capital, Columbus, and other areas in the state are becoming increasingly appealing to investors. Ohio-based venture capital funds raised nearly a billion dollars in capital between 2013 and 2018, and in 2016, $470 million was invested in over 200 startups in the state. Not surprisingly, Kauffman rates Columbus as one of the top U.S. metro areas for scaling young companies. And almost half of the

U.S. population is within a day's drive of Columbus (perhaps contributing to its flyover status). [187]

Entrepreneurs in Ohio have access to many entrepreneurial and networking events as well as incubators and accelerators. For example, Techstars, a worldwide entrepreneurial network, hosts Startup Week Columbus, a free, five-day "celebration of community" to build momentum and opportunities for entrepreneurs.[188]

Ohio State University is home to a Center for Innovation and Entrepreneurship that provides opportunities for students and hosts competitions for best business plan and Best of Student Startups (BOSS).[189] The Better Business Bureau in Central Ohio also hosts an award ceremony to honor millennial entrepreneurial organizations.[191] Private organizations are involved and encourage entrepreneurship through events, including the Ohio Entrepreneur Expo (hosted by Startup Mag) and Venture Dinner, an awards ceremony and networking event sponsored by VentureOhio, an organization created to foster a collaborative ecosystem, provide access to capital, and tell Ohio's story.[192]

Kansas City Region – Show me the Stars

In 2011, the Kansas City Chamber of Commerce announced their goal of "making Kansas City America's most entrepreneurial city." Supporting entrepreneurship was one aspect of their "Big 5" initiative, and they have devoted extensive resources to make this happen.[193] As a result, they have experienced a surge in startups in recent years and people are taking note. The online bank GoBankingRates included it among the top five best cities to start a business in a 2019[194] survey, and the Kansas City metropolitan area was ranked 15th by WalletHub for starting a business in

2018. It is also considered a top city for millennial entrepreneurs. [195]

KCSourceLink shares the Chamber of Commerce's goal. They act as a connector for small businesses and entrepreneurs and resources in virtually every area they may need. They created a comprehensive annual entrepreneurship report and posted a dashboard identifying daily regional classes and events that canvas topics including business planning and growth, sales and marketing, taxes, and networking opportunities. There are also 1 Million Cups events in the city.[195]The Chamber also hosts events, networking opportunities, and awards ceremonies.

In conjunction with universities throughout the state, the Missouri Department of Economic Development created an Innovation Center Network. These physical locations offer access to expertise and specialized resources.[196] Kansas City hosts a Global Entrepreneurship Week and Techweek, celebrating technology and entrepreneurship, and they facilitate events for specific groups such as women or young entrepreneurs. A case study on St. Louis as a startup ecosystem found that events hosted by other support organizations, such as the Center for Emerging Technologies and co-located grant recipients, served as catalysts for meeting other entrepreneurs who may not otherwise meet. The study also identified four events run by volunteers that were attended by many entrepreneurs: Startup Weekend, Start Louis, Build Guild, and Code Until Dawn.[198]

Are there any common characteristics about these events?

The range and diversity of the programs and events available in emerging flyover ecosystems show the commitment of their entrepreneurial infrastructure. Although the culture of the communities and entrepreneurial ecosystems are unique to each region, there are events and programs shared across these and other systems that can serve as a framework for budding systems. Consider the following options when developing a support structure within your entrepreneurial community.

Don't do it alone:

A required characteristic of an entrepreneurial ecosystem is community-wide support from a range of stakeholders: existing small and large businesses; local, regional, and state governments; financial institutions; and other entrepreneurs, just to name a few. These ecosystem members come with a wealth of invaluable knowledge and are just waiting for an invitation to share it. Who better to talk about tax issues than with an accountant? A tutorial from a city government representative can save someone a day or more in trying to decipher required forms and paperwork. National and international support organizations like the Kauffman Foundation, TechStars, StartupNation, and Pipeline are great resources for identifying issues – and solutions – relevant to entrepreneurs.

No need to reinvent the wheel:

There are literally hundreds of programs and events hosted every day by different groups, from offering personal advice or business information to startup weekends and boot camps. Chambers of Commerce, universities, associations, libraries, Meetup groups and dozens of other organizations post calendars of events a few weeks or months in advance. These represent different formats, times of day, duration, venues, and topics, providing something for everyone if you're willing to do a little research. Some groups are informal and meet for coffee while others host more structured meetings and events. There are also state-level and national programs, such as 1 Million Cups, directed at entrepreneurial growth.

Offer breadth and depth: As seen in these examples, programs are available on virtually every topic an entrepreneur might need to learn or develop from creating a business plan to finding capital to marketing and networking to scaling a business and going public. And speaking of virtually, don't forget about webinars, MOOCs (massive open online courses), TED Talks, LinkedIn groups and other online opportunities to become better informed on broad and niche issues.

Collaborate with entrepreneurs:

Family and friends are great sources of support, but knowing others who have successfully faced similar challenges can make all the difference in bringing an idea to reality. Events hosted by entrepreneurs for entrepreneurs is a must for all ecosystems. No one knows better the joy of acquiring a first round of funding or the despair of another prototype disappointment than someone who has lived the experience. Events pairing entrepreneurs combine learning and networking opportunities and, because many angel investors are entrepreneurs in their local communities, these events present the potential for financing.

Show and tell:

The events noted here focus on programs that provide information to entrepreneurs. However, as every entrepreneur knows, there's nothing quite like jumping in and doing something firsthand to embrace the experience. In addition to being an audience member, entrepreneurs can also create awareness and interest by being a participant at various events. Speaking at schools and or community events promotes entrepreneurship and community-building. Additionally, many groups offer awards for different entrepreneurial-related efforts. Self-nominating is a great way to promote an innovation with the added benefit of networking at the award ceremony. Entrepreneurs who may not be ready to submit their own projects can show their support for others by nominating someone else.

How can you avoid "innovation theater" and "professional accelerator attendees"?

Many organizations make an attempt at entrepreneurialism by hosting "innovation labs" or some other Shark Tank-like opportunity. However, these efforts too often reflect a moment in time rather than a planned process or allocation of necessary resources. As a result, participants get caught up in the excitement of developing a great idea and product without the critical foundation of understanding the importance of a viable business model. The Startup Junkie / Conductor experience has shown that TechStars' Startup Weekend format can be a valuable "top of funnel" exercise to get new ventures created through an efficient ideation process. In 54 hours, 8-10 new possible ventures are present. In the several years Startup Junkie has run these events, at least one viable startup was created per cohort. Companies such as More Technologies (a pioneer in education robotics) and RaftUp are notable examples. Beyond the ventures created, the connections made between founders and technologists in a Startup Weekend are crucial to the future venture creation that definitely occurs after a Startup Weekend has concluded.

However, some participants become frustrated because they believed that their company supported another's ideas, yet their company doesn't get developed. Alternatively, a participant might take their positive feedback as confirmation of their imminent success and look for an accelerator program. Without a strong foundation, however, they are not likely to find funding, so they bounce from program to program wondering why no one is seizing the opportunity in front of them.

Steve Blank, known as the Father of Modern Entrepreneurship, refers to this phenomenon as "innovation theater" – the effect when businesses jump on the entrepreneurial bandwagon because innovation is the current buzz and it makes the company feel like they're on the cutting-edge. Banks, an entrepreneur eight times over and proponent of the "lean startup" movement, studies organizations to understand why their innovation programs work, or -- as is more often the case -- don't work. Based on his observations he has identified a few key reasons why innovation theater is more harm than help.

In many cases, companies provide an outpost for teams to develop their products. When they come to the home office, however, their projects are no longer priorities. Instead, their efforts are preempted by business as usual. It often turns out that there were never any metrics for evaluation and no money in the budget to build and execute any projects that don't support the existing business model, let alone create a pipeline to support ongoing innovation.[199] As a result, these efforts become costly non-starters that deter creative minds from offering new solutions.

Other obstacles to true innovation include a lack of direction and appropriate resources. Teams are sent off with instructions to "go innovate" but without guidance on what business gaps need to be addressed or connection to resources to help direct their process.[199] They may get put in a newly renovated space with the latest in ergonomic seating and white board technology when a round table, a stack of sticky notes, and clear direction would do the trick.[201] There is a misplaced emphasis on what looks good on the outside rather than what works best on the inside. Moreover, a recent Harvard Business School study made the assertion with some evidence that open space office layouts designed to facilitate collaboration were actually a drag on productivity.

Building a space and providing tools are a start, but those factors aren't enough to build a program. Steve Blank notes the differences between innovators — those who invent a new product, service, or process – and entrepreneurs — those who can move an innovation through adoption and delivery within the organization's existing company policy. Both types of people are essential to a successful innovation team. Teams need to be educated on the different elements of a business plan and how to research and test their ideas. Emphasizing processes over a single goal such as "winning" a demo-day provides more realistic experiences and expectations and shows greater commitment from the organization.[202]

Similarly, teams should have a sense of what to innovate and how they can make things easier for end users. Leaders should provide clearly defined methods for teaching and measuring innovation — the how, what, when, why, and who should be understood by everyone on the team from the outset. They should also look for both innovative and entrepreneurial talent among their workforce, within and beyond their own teams. If an organization is committed to fostering innovation, recognition such as bonuses and awards should be linked to it.[202] As with all entrepreneurial systems, shared initiatives and transparency are important. As an ecosystem builder, you can share the importance of building a company on a strong foundation and provide learning opportunities from other entrepreneurs who can share their experience of being truly innovative in their business.

CHAPTER 10:

Building the Mentor Base

What is an ecosystem mentor?

With good reason, the first of the four pillars of a thriving ecosystem is talent. While much of our discussion has focused on entrepreneurs and potential employees, the support of mentors is also critical to the success of an ecosystem. Mentors provide insights on the entrepreneurship process and professional and personal support through the ups and downs of navigating that process. Access to several well-respected mentors is essential to entrepreneurial and ecosystem growth.[204] As a testament to the beneficial influence of mentors, remember that 70% of new businesses that are mentored survive longer than five years.[204]

Ecosystem mentors have valuable experience and knowledge and act as advisors and confidants for startup founders. Based on a survey of thirty-three entrepreneurial programs across the United States, researcher Jeffery Sanchez-Burks suggests that an effective mentor is someone who:

» inspires curiosity;

» challenges assumptions and expectations;

» guides through asking probing questions;

» is honest and direct about what he or she doesn't know; and

» is eager to learn alongside the mentee.[205]

Mentors are a vital resource for entrepreneurs because they literally give away their experience! They know and understand the challenges founders face because they have been through it already. If a new crisis arises, they can call on a network of equally or differently qualified associates. Mentors understand what it takes to run a business and can help prioritize tasks and goals and offer a boost when things become overwhelming.

Research indicates that entrepreneurs learn the most from mentors who also are or were experienced entrepreneurs and businesspeople.[207] This is not surprising, as the biggest knowledge gap for many startups is a lack of experience. Fortunately, entrepreneurs comprise the greatest number of mentors. Unfortunately, mentor availability remains a challenge, especially within organizations. This has the potential of producing negative outcomes because mentorship programs may feel pressured to relax their required qualifications for participation in an effort to increase the number of members.[208] As such, both mentors and mentees should take the time to identify a match that is a good fit and will lead to a trusted relationship.

How might a founder go about seeking, engaging, and properly leveraging a mentor?

Potential entrepreneurs are everywhere. The U.S. Small Business Association has several programs that include mentoring services. They partner with SCORE to connect small businesses with mentors, and their Veterans Business Outreach Center offers mentoring services to veterans, transitioning service members, and National Guard and Reserve Members and their wives. SBA also runs Small Business Development Centers across the country that offer free business consulting services.[209] Corporate employers and universities also often provide resources to match founders and mentors. From an entrepreneur's point of view and for their own good, they need to do significant due diligence on a potential mentor. These people are seldom attached to SCORE or the Small Business Development Centers. Many times these organizations have career corporate executives with lots of solid enterprise experience and no clue about the realities of building a business from scratch. Resources from these sources would be better categorized as subject matter experts (SMEs) and not venture-ready mentors.

Joining an association or special interest group is a great way to meet like-minded people. Local business and networking events offer the company of diverse groups who may be looking for a new opportunity for engagement. They can also look to their own contacts and friends of friends who may have an interest in their project.[210] Ecosystem builders can strengthen their own networks and connect with potential entrepreneurial mentors. One easy strategy is to connect through LinkedIn and reacquaint oneself with the many interesting people one has met at conferences and other events throughout the years.

Why should an ecosystem builder train founders to properly identify, engage, and leverage the capabilities of a mentor?

Mentors are good for business and it is well worth the effort an entrepreneur might expend to find one. Various studies support the positive impact of mentorship in improving career outcomes for individuals.[211] For example:

»   93% of startups report that mentorship is instrumental to success;[212]

»   Founders mentored by top-performing entrepreneurs are three times more likely to become top performers themselves;[213]

»   80% of CEOs receive some form of mentorship; and

»   89% of small business owners without a mentor wish they had one.[214]

While formal mentoring programs can be a good option for entrepreneurs who may be new to a community or industry, research finds that informal mentoring has a much more significant effect on career outcomes than formal mentoring. [215] Ideally, founders should seek multiple mentors to help them learn and grow in many ways. Jack Welch, former CEO of General Electric and the current Executive Chairperson of The Jack Welch Management Institute, advises young people to "see everyone as a mentor" and to find people they admire in different areas of expertise (e.g., public speaking, leadership, accounting) to be mentors in those area to help them expand their skill set across different domains.[216]

Mentees often cite guidance by mentors as the most important factor contributing to their success. Mentorship is most appreciated when it comes to the review of business documents (e.g., business plans, pitch decks), active involvement in the business, and introductions to partners and networking.[217]

What are the best practices for entrepreneurial ecosystem mentors?

Most mentoring programs lack support, planning, and budgeting,[218] so there are few ideal models to follow. But some programs do provide outstanding examples of best practices. For example, the Mowgli Foundation, a non-profit mentoring organization in Africa and the Middle East, exists on the belief that mentoring makes all the difference between the answer to the region's economic challenges or the poverty that contributes to it. Mowgli has a six-month mentor training program to prepare mentors for their role and a more niche program for microfinance institutions and loan officers. Their 12-month Entrepreneur Mentoring Program is designed for both mentors and entrepreneurs to provide a foundation for a mutually-rewarding, long-term relationship. It includes phases for mentoring awareness and program overview, a time to prepare for matching, a three-day workshop during which matches are made and agreements defined, and ongoing supervision with periodic refresher sessions. Program alumni are encouraged to stay involved after they complete the program and to continue their good work by mentoring others.[219]

Their approach is working. Based on 20 years of data, Mowgli has identified critical outcomes that can contribute to best practices for ecosystem mentors. Below are some highlights of their "mentoring effect"[220]:

» their entrepreneurs contributed $18.4 million to the region's economy by creating and safeguarding of over 3,400 jobs;

» 89% of entrepreneurs' businesses remained operational;

» 81% of entrepreneurs felt more confident;

» 85% of mentors felt they could better empathize and understand others; and

» investors in the region achieved an average Return on Mentoring Investment of 890%.

Another highly successful program was created by Permjot Valia and is called MentorCamp. This is a multi-day, intensive mentor speed-dating process that gets viable ventures exposure to a cross section of mentors from around the world. This initial MentorCamp process leads to long-term relationships and in many cases builds the networks of both the founders and the mentors. MentorCamp events have been held in Canada, the US, and South Africa.

What are the differences between "mentors" and "subject matter experts"?

Entrepreneurs and entrepreneurship are concepts often used synonymously with other terms such as subject matter experts and coaches. While these roles are related, they are distinct and can be characterized by the role, goals, and length of the relationship.[221]

Mentors are trusted associates who provide advice to help the mentee's professional growth and performance, and they act as a role model to support the mentee. Their focus is on the mentee -- the founder of the business -- and their contributions are broad and based on the founder's need. On the other hand, subject matter experts (SMEs) are experts in a defined and specific area such as finance, marketing, or law. Accordingly, they focus on helping an entrepreneur with issues related to their expertise. This

130

may require only a few meetings or perhaps a longer-term relationship, though typically on an as-needed basis.[222]

Some SMEs also work with entrepreneurs as business coaches. The coach role is more prescriptive and focused on performance. They help founders strategize a solution to an identified challenge. Their relationship generally lasts for the duration of the issue being addressed.[223] Each role contributes to the business, but it is important to be able to distinguish between them and seek the appropriate counsel for your needs.

What are the expectations of a mentor?

The value of mentorship to entrepreneurs is well established, but a good mentor/mentee relationship should be two-way. Entrepreneurs must remember that they are responsible for their own development, including the relationships that support them.[224] No one is more invested in the success of the project than founders, so they should take time to identify their needs and then meet with several people to find a good fit, or as Jack Welch recommends, several good fits.

Many mentors cite "giving back" as their motivation, but it is still important for mentees to recognize that although mentors are wise, they are not omnipotent. When a mentor has agreed to support an entrepreneur, it is important for both parties to set realistic expectations. This might include guidelines for how much time each party is able to give and communication (e.g., can the mentee call at any time or are scheduled dates better?).[225] Furthermore, although mentors are the senior person in the relationship, it is not their responsibility to manage it. Mentees should take the initiative to identify objectives and to check in and schedule time together. In return, good mentors recognize their role as an advisor and source of support. They should help mentees assess and address their objectives without criticism or imposing their preferred approach.

Mentors appreciate having a high-quality relationship with their mentee, being utilized effectively, and engaging in reciprocal learning.[226] Mentors may have greater business knowledge than the new founder, but there might be an area of expertise the mentee can share such as suggestions for a new app, recommendations for accommodations in another city, or advice on a hobby or common interest.

Founders can supplement the advice of their mentors with virtual mentor advice. Founders who admire well-known entrepreneurs can become an SMEs on a favorite role model. People like Oprah Winfrey, Steve Jobs, and Elon Musk are household names with books, articles, and movies made about them. Newspapers, business magazines, and academic journals offer extensive coverage on top entrepreneurs, allowing followers to read about their background and challenges, learn their process, and assess their methods. This provides another perspective for the entrepreneur's vision.

Founders are well served to take inputs from multiple mentors and SMEs with a diversity of experience. Even the best mentors, who religiously follow a good Socratic process with a mentee, will bring their own biases to every conversation. The founder's task is to then synthesize their own view of truth based on all of those inputs. This sort of approach (a finely tuned founder-filter) will limit mentor whiplash and will force the founder to develop a keen ability to synthesize and validate the truths about their business model and strategy. The best mentors will appreciate follow up conversations from founders who convey critical thinking, relay the multiple mentor inputs they received, and communicate the direction they ultimately followed. The best mentors understand that founders must follow their own path, and the mentor's job is to illuminate the way, advise of the risks, and then allow the founder to walk the walk themselves. Ecosystem builders can help to facilitate mentor and mentee relationships through community engagement events that allow for networking and connecting interested parties.

CHAPTER 11:

Networking

What is networking and why is it important to the entrepreneurial ecosystem?

In earlier chapters we have iterated the importance of networking as a central entrepreneurial responsibility. Let's take a step back and consider what networking entails and why it is so important to the entrepreneurial ecosystem.

First, a definition: networking is developing and using contacts made through people you know and others you have met at business-related events for a reason other than the initial meeting.[226] For example, you might participate in National Entrepreneur's Day (on the third Tuesday in November) panel about startups at a local school and meet another panelist whose business concept complements an entrepreneur in your ecosystem. You connect the two, who meet for coffee later that week and decide to share vendor and customer lists so that both can expand their distribution. Your and the entrepreneur from your community have extended your networks by one.

Having a network is important to all professionals (and all people). Entrepreneurs in particular need a strong network because they start from the ground up. Someone who develops a new idea for a Fortune 500 company has a built-in network. They can call on supervisors, support staff, colleagues, partners, and the tens or hundreds of others who interact with the many facets of the business. A startup might be one or two people for the first few years, but they still need a support infrastructure, and networking is the way to build it.

As entrepreneurs share their ideas with friends and family, they are likely to hear comments like, "My sister-in-law works with a guy who used to do that – I'll give you his number!" This is the beginning of the professional network: friends of friends, former co-workers and classmates, neighbors, in-laws, and the person in the next seat at National Entrepreneurs Day. The potential to meet someone with whom a mutually beneficial relationship can grow is everywhere!

Ecosystem builders also benefit from developing a network — it is vital to the life of the entire community. Entrepreneurial innovations fill gaps but they are of no use if the entrepreneur doesn't have the resources to bring it to market or if the people who can benefit from their ideas are unaware of them. Knowing just one person who can make a connection or set up a meeting can make all the difference. Angels and other investors are always on the watch for an innovation that fits within their portfolio, and sharing a table at an event or award ceremony might position you to connect one of these funders to an entrepreneur in your network.

When an ecosystem builder develops their network, there are two important groups that should be included: mentors and entrepreneurs. It may seem obvious, but it is tempting for an ecosystem builder to grow their network with community leaders, other ecosystem builders, or subject matter experts. While those groups are important, the ecosystem must be centered around entrepreneurs, and mentors must be included to help guide and support the startup endeavours. These two groups have the clearest understanding of the challenges, fears, "a-ha" moments, and opportunities for starting and scaling a company. Lastly, sharing resources and contacts demonstrate the connectedness of the ecosystem and help ensure its longevity.

What are some of the best practices involved in creating a thriving network of entrepreneurs?[228]

In chapter 10 we identified various programs and events that provide opportunities for entrepreneurial networking and development. Here we offer more specific approaches and behaviors that ecosystem builders can use to maximize entrepreneurial networking opportunities.

Have a plan:

Developing your professional contacts is essential, and networking is how it is done. To make the most of your efforts, take time to develop a plan. Consider your goals and what you want to achieve. Think about which entrepreneurs you want to know and the best opportunities to meet them. Look for opportunities to connect others within your ecosystem, including entrepreneurial competitors, to maintain neutrality and inclusivity. Also think about your role in the community and how you can give back in a meaningful way that is important to you.

Be intentional and selective:

Time is the most valuable asset an ecosystem builder has. Local events are important, but don't let mileage dictate your networking circle. Become familiar with organizations in your region and the types of events they host. Take advantage of sources that provide calendars of events weeks in advance so you can schedule time for networking.

Networking is two-way:

Finding like-minded others who support entrepreneurship is critical to the growth and success of the ecosystem. Equally important is being a source of support for others. When looking for events that will help you better position your business, also look for opportunities to be of service. You might mentor a college student or give a presentation on an area of expertise at a library or senior center. Sponsoring a sports team or town event is a great way to show support and generate some publicity. Think about what you hope to gain from networking and offer that same opportunity to someone else through a great introduction or problem-solving advice.

Develop networking skills:

Some people are at home in any social situation, but a far greater number dread having to meet new people and talk about themselves. Preparation and practice go a long way in alleviating anxiety and focusing your comments.

Practice your pitch:

No one knows you better than you, but when it comes to talking about ourselves we can become flustered. Besides your name and occupation, think of three things you would like someone new to know about you. Align your bio with the event and the goals you hope to achieve. That is, rather than talking about your children and how much you love snowboarding, express your interest in the speaker or topic, talk about a great business book or article you read, and share a new technology or trend in the field.

Be concise:

Be able to answer "boilerplate" questions about your job and ecosystem-building in one or two sentences. Also, be considerate when responding to questions. Be thoughtful and responsive, but don't go into excessive detail. Someone can always ask a question if they need more information.

Take the plunge:

Every new day brings a new opportunity, so embrace the chance to add to your network and learn something new. Arm yourself with a name tag and business cards and take the first step. If you think the situation will be too stressful, recruit a friend to go with you to your first few events to increase your comfort and confidence level.

Be authentic and be yourself:

While your mother's admonishment to "behave!" still holds, it shouldn't be at the expense of you being you. You are your own greatest asset and the best representative of your business. Professional acquaintances are great but creating a friendship can create a lifelong bond.

Talk to everyone...:

Don't be the person sitting alone at a table looking at your phone while waiting for an event to start. Make — and reach — a goal to meet five new people at every event. Find a newcomer or someone standing alone and introduce yourself, then introduce that person to someone you know. Also, introduce yourself to the event hosts and ask them to make other introductions for you. When it comes time to sit down, find new people to meet and engage with them after the event by asking their views on the speaker or topic.

...but be sure to listen:

Ask people why they came to the event and see if there is a way for you to support their goals. Also, have a list of questions ready to engage new contacts. Inquiring about their connection to the organization, how they became involved in their field, who inspired them, where they went to school or how they learned their business, can stimulate a conversation and reveal common experiences.

Follow-up:

Events may be one-and-done, but the goal of networking is to build a relationship, so follow-up should be central to your plan. Send a note after a meeting with a link to a great article they can use or an invitation to meet for coffee. If someone mentioned an area of interest, keep an eye out for information (or do some research yourself) and share it. If an event or organization closely mirrors your own goals and beliefs, follow-up there, as well. See if there is an opportunity to be involved as a guest speaker, sponsor, or board member.

How can social media be used to expand a network?

While community events provide many opportunities to meet new people, social media offers extensive opportunities to reach multiple audiences at no or low cost for an ecosystem builder to expand their network. The same is true for entrepreneurs.

Social media marketing tips are one of the most frequently asked questions of entrepreneurial support organizations. There are so many social media channels and options that it can be difficult for an entrepreneur to navigate. When helping an entrepreneur with their social media strategy, it is important to emphasize the need for clarity in content and audience and to remind them that social media is supposed to be social - that is, a conversation *with* customers, not a sales pitch *at* them. They should be authentic and transparent and create a dialogue. Many businesses incorporate various methods to get customers to "like" their site, but this is a poor measure of success. In too many cases, "likes" are "bought" in exchange for an incentive such as a discounted rate or inclusion in a giveaway. This overvalues followers. Responses to individual posts, including comments, shares, and likes are better metrics because they reflect user engagement.[229] That is, it means a user actually viewed and reflected on the content versus clicking a like button or answering random questions to receive perks.

Ecosystem builders also benefit from using social media to grow their network and highlight the many assets of their community. It is a great way to support an entrepreneurial culture and interact with local talent. However, it is beneficial to know the difference between the many social media options and the best way to utilize them to their fullest potential. Facebook continues to dominate social media across age and gender with 68% of adults using it.[229] To maximize effectiveness on Facebook and all social media channels, segment your audiences and offer customized content to post during their peak viewing times on each respective platform (don't forget to consider time differences between east and west coast). Facebook viewers, for example, check in as they start their day around 9 a.m., and then again around noon when they're getting ready for lunch. If you know someone under the age of twenty, you know that they are night owls, so content targeted at this demographic should be scheduled accordingly.

While it is not a traditional social media platform, the video-sharing site YouTube dominates social media with 73% of U.S. adults reporting that they use it.[230] Beyond cat videos and celebrity stalking, YouTube is useful for tutorials and other how-to demonstrations. It is frequently cited as second only to Google as a popular search engine, even though it's technically not a search engine. With more than 300 hours of video uploaded to the site every minute,[231] competition for views is high. Still, it can serve as a repository for your video, which you can link via another site.

Instagram continues to grow in popularity with roughly 35% of American adults using it.[233] It is favored for picture sharing, so clothing, jewelry, food, and other industries that offer visually pleasing products do well on this platform. Instagram, like many other apps, is meant for use on mobile devices, so be sure to preview content on various devices before posting to ensure it appears the way you want it to.

Twitter was originally designed for short messages of 140 characters but has since doubled that allowable character amount. Favored by celebrities, about 45% of Americans use Twitter,[234] most of them under the age of 29. Another favorite among younger audiences is Snapchat - about 78% of 18- to 24-year-olds use this channel.[235]

LinkedIn is known as a professional site and is used primarily for business connection purposes. It is popular with college graduates and affluent households, and about half its users have a college degree.[236]

Bill Gate's claim that "content is king"[237] still holds true, and an ecosystem builder should consider content with their own social media strategy. Content is for the benefit of your audience, so make it relevant and entertaining to them. Spend some time developing a content schedule and calendar that reflects what the ecosystem wants and needs. Develop a consistent voice across all your messaging and align content with your industry or business. Informative posts can be educational or entertaining, or you can post a quote or video. Curating content from other sources saves time and can increase your viewership through relationships with others who enjoy the material. Include questions or a poll in several posts to engage viewers and encourage feedback.

Networking is one of the most vital ways to strengthen the ecosystem and provide connections and resources for entrepreneurs. Relationships can be cultivated through in-person events, and reputations can be validated through social media interaction. As you continue to grow and strengthen your ecosystem, remember that at the end of the day an ecosystem builder's purpose is to support entrepreneurs. The network you accumulate is ultimately for the benefit of supporting the small business community.

PART 4:

Tools of
the Trade

CHAPTER 12:

Venture Ecosystem Building Canvas

The most successful ecosystems all contain elements of the four pillars: talent, culture, community engagement, and capital. However, for those communities that are in the early stages of creating a desirable place for startups, it can seem daunting to know where to begin to cultivate the development of the pillars. To help community leaders and entrepreneurs start these conversations, the Startup Junkie and Conductor teams have created a strategy to identify and leverage community advantages that support entrepreneurship at little or no cost.

Following the tenants of Asset Based Community Development,[237] the Venture Ecosystem Building Canvas is designed to identify the innovative and entrepreneurial strengths that are already present in a community and then determine what people or organizations exist that can help to amplify those strengths. This type of approach was first brought into the mainstream by Greg Horowitt and Victor Hwang through their Rainforest Canvas, a series of questions categorized into nine dimensions focused on innovation leaders. The Startup Junkie and Conductor teams have taken this approach one step further by incorporating the Strategic Doing methodology of identifying, linking, and leveraging community resources before implementing an action plan.[238] Through more than a decade's worth of experience, we have discovered that resources and partner organizations usually already exist in a community, but it is up to an entrepreneurial champion to pull all the pieces together and initiate change.

The Venture Ecosystem Building Canvas includes an assessment of the four pillars of talent, culture, capital, and community engagement. Below is a list of questions included in the canvas. They are not intended to be all-encompassing; they are designed to provide a framework for thinking about the components of a given entrepreneurial ecosystem. The Full Venture Ecosystem Building Canvas can be found in Appendix A.

Talent	*Culture*
1. Who are the local innovators, inventors, or entrepreneurs who have built successful products, services, or companies?	1. What kinds of innovative social networks already exist that could be leveraged, and what is the cadence of existing events, workshops, and programs?
2. Who champions innovation and entrepreneurship in K-12?	2. What small businesses have generations of influence in the community?
3. What support organizations exist for the purpose of helping entrepreneurs?	3. What well-known amenities exist in the community that contribute to the culture and attract and retain talent?

4. What colleges or universities exist within or in close proximity to our community?	4. How is the community plugged into global innovation and entrepreneurial initiatives?
5. What coding, data science, or STEM programs exist in close proximity to our community?	5. What role are successful entrepreneurs playing in mentoring and investing in startups?
6. What non-traditional workforce training is available?	6. What successful existing community initiatives have been launched within the past two years?
7. What public, private, governmental research or innovation labs are in close proximity to our community?	7. What is the leading cause of community initiatives to succeed?
8. What's the level of maturity of the entrepreneurship and commercialization programs at the local university or college, as evidenced by student and faculty spin-outs, licensed IPs, and public and private funds raised?	8. How receptive and welcoming is the community to new ideas?
9. How is the business acumen of those in arts and culture being strengthened to increase the creative economy?	9. How diverse is the community in terms of demographics, beliefs, and experiences?

10. When ventures were successfully exited in the past, what was the economic impact and what did the successful entrepreneurs do next?	10. What "loosely organized" or organic activities are going on?

Community Engagement	Capital
1. What industries and competencies is the community most known for?	1. What financial resources are available to fund new initiatives?
2. What flagship enterprises exist within these industries?	2. What capital is available to invest in new ventures (angels, angel funds, VCs)?
3. What needs do the flagship enterprises have that small businesses, entrepreneurs, or new initiatives can serve?	3. What's the level of angel or early-stage "Investor Acumen" among the community?
4. Who are the entrepreneurial leaders, business leaders, and municipal leaders in the community with the reputation, commitment, experience and resources to lead a new initiative?	4. What lending programs are available for non-traditional borrowers (e.g. low credit, criminal history)?
5. Which organizations are willing to come together to serve as organizational champions for a new initiative?	5. Is there any SBIR/STTR support available?

6. What space is available for events/training, co-working, scale-up, or other programming?	6. What other types of desirable capital is available (e.g. social, natural, built, etc.)?
7. What resources are available out of town that entrepreneurs travel to obtain and how can those be replicated?	7. How have new initiatives been funded in the past?
8. What is the view towards risk taking in the broader community?	8. What technical assistance programs are available to assist financial management?
9. Are there any "pockets" of expertise that could be leveraged?	9. Who is helping entrepreneurs become investment ready?
10. What is the "Leadership Climate" among the various leadership groups in the community (city leaders, chamber leaders, economic development leaders, etc.)?	10. What financial institution is the most knowledgeable in SBA backed loans?

Answer those questions as thoroughly as possible, and write the actual names of entrepreneurs, corporations, and leaders listed. This is not a time to be vague and general but to really nail down the specific assets that make a community ripe for ecosystem development.

After you have answered the questions and exhausted any additional discussion, it is time to reflect on the standouts of each pillar. What emerged as the strongest response to the questions? For example, the assessment may have revealed that there are three colleges and universities within 50 miles of a community (Talent Question #4), the headquarters of a CDFI is located in the community (Capital Question #4), there is an active mentorship program (Culture Question #5), and a strong industry is trucking and logistics (Community Engagement Question #1).

The next step is to think about how all of these things can be combined into a new community initiative that encourages and grows entrepreneurship. Perhaps your community needs a new mentoring program with leaders in logistics to work with low-income college students on a new invention or venture that supports the trucking industry with seed funding provided by the CDFI. There are countless combinations on how new ideas and initiatives can bubble to the surface, but the key is to focus on what a community already has instead of what it is lacking.

Lastly, one of the most important components of the Venture Ecosystem Building Canvas is the storytelling component. Positive, frequent stories of entrepreneurs and their achievements helps to increase momentum and change the perception of the ecosystem. As news travels of the entrepreneurial happenings in a community, talent will flock to where the action is, and the local reputation will start to shift as innovative activities increase. There are many ways to tell the story of an entrepreneur or an innovative initiative, including traditional media outlets and social media channels. Startup Junkie has a podcast that highlights the local entrepreneurs and tells the stories of their creations and successes.[239] The podcast platform has also been a great way to form relationships with business leaders and government officials as they are invited on the show to talk about their initiatives. Once the entrepreneurial stories are told more frequently with increasing richness of content, the media outlets will soon start seeking the entrepreneur out instead of the other way around!

CHAPTER 13

Strategic Initiative Planning Process

Some communities have independent entrepreneurial champions who collaborate with multiple groups to kick-start ecosystem building practices. Other communities have whole organizations focused on growing and supporting entrepreneurship and entrepreneurial activities. No matter the size of the leading organization, once the Venture Ecosystem Canvas is complete and entrepreneurial initiatives are outlined, a Strategic Initiative Planning Process is needed to create a clear path forward. Effective planning is a critical component of optimum, sustainable growth, and without a focused plan, organizations of all sizes and independent ecosystem builders are apt to drift from one initiative to another, not knowing what the end result will look like or even if it has been accomplished.

The Strategic Initiative Planning Process developed by the Startup Junkie and Conductor teams was inspired by Tony Jeary's work in strategic acceleration.[241] His book of the same name says achievement of any goals, plans, or strategies effectively requires three predicates. Our planning process has adapted Jeary's definitions, based on our own experience in the field of ecosystem building:

1. **Clarity** – the ability to get crystal clear about the purpose and direction of your initiative or organization, as well as clarity about the desired outcomes you or you wish to achieve.

2. **Focus** — the development of a laser-like guidance system in order to avoid distraction and to concentrate on the high-leverage activities that will produce the greatest results.

3. **Execution** — the ability to effectively deploy and direct resources in order to achieve the desired outcomes.

At the end of the day, strong, sustainable growth of a business, an organization or an ecosystem-building initiative does not happen by accident. It happens because the right actions are taken at the right time, in the right way, to produce a desired, sustainable outcome. This requires leadership. Leaders are responsible for ensuring that clarity, focus and impeccable execution exist in any organization they have been entrusted to lead. Failure to do so is an abdication-leadership responsibility. When leaders ensure there is clarity of purpose and direction, when they remove distractions by saying "no" to certain possible actions or courses of action, and when they properly allocate resources toward the desired outcomes that have been identified, they have drastically increased their organization's or initiative's probability of success.

In the daily practice of Startup Junkie and the Conductor, coaching, consulting, and training is provided to entrepreneurs, business executives, and organizational leaders across a wide variety of industries, spanning a wide range of sizes. From startups to well-established firms, from colleges and universities to Fortune 100s, most seem to struggle with this concept of strategic initiative planning. How do we properly implement our plans? How do we anticipate so many unknowns? How do we determine the best actions to take in an economic climate that is changing so rapidly? These are some of the questions that are routinely asked as leaders are engaged in venture ecosystem building. A solid plan does not remove all of the potential ambiguities in doing business. A solid plan provides a framework through which to face and deal with those ambiguities. Leadership judgment is still required amidst the myriad of unanticipated events, hurdles, and roadblocks that spring up after a solid venture ecosystem plan is created and agreed upon.

While some leaders and their organizations have the ability to create high-quality plans organically, others require some degree of outside assistance to ensure the highest quality output. A skilled, neutral, outside facilitator can improve the quality of any planning exercise. These facilitators draw on a wealth of experience across multiple organizations and can ask the difficult questions that might remain unasked in an organic planning process.

There is a tendency to be overly verbose in planning exercises and the resulting plan documents. However, a well-crafted plan is an exercise in subtraction, not addition, and it is certainly not an exercise in multiplication! After the Venture Ecosystem Canvas is complete, the Strategic Initiative Planning Process should focus on seven key ingredients, all of which can usually fit on a handful of pages. How you discover those key ingredients is part of the "secret sauce" of a quality planning exercise. Once it is created, the positive outcomes on your community or organization can be dramatic. The following terms are points for an individual or an organization to ponder as they consider their role in building an entrepreneurial ecosystem.

The full Strategic Initiative Planning Process can be found in Appendix B.

Mission — This is why your organization or ecosystem-building initiative exists. It describes what it was created to do, ideally from the perspective of your entrepreneurs or key stakeholders – the primary beneficiaries of your efforts.

Vision — This is a specific point in the future, a destination, usually three to five years out, that the organization or initiative aspires to achieve or at which you aspire to arrive. The keys to remember in articulating a quality vision is that it must be aspirational, time-bound, and compelling, and it must have absolute clarity.

Values — The shared values of an organization/initiative describe its desired culture. They serve as the behavioral compass, or the behavior guardrails, as you execute against your Mission and as you drive toward the fulfillment of your Vision. Shared Values are the beliefs that you and your team believe so deeply in that they directly impact your individual and collective behavior.

Long-term Targets — Also sometimes called "strategic objectives," we prefer to call them "long-term targets" because they span the same time frame as your Vision, and they are specific and measurable. A leader should be able to look back at the appointed time and answer definitively as to whether the targets were achieved or not. Ideally, organizations should only pursue a handful (usually three to five, maybe seven in larger organizations) of long-term targets.

Short-term Goals — These are the handful (again, usually three to five but maybe up to seven in larger organizations) of very specific things that must be achieved in the following 12 months to ensure you remain on track toward your long-term targets and ultimately the fulfillment of your Vision. If you picked a date five years out for your long-term targets, then these goals must take you 20 percent of the way there in the following year. If you selected a date three years out, your short-term goals must get you one-third of the way there within the next year.

Key Performance Indicators — Your key performance indicators (KPIs) are the handful of things (no more than five to seven) that you should be measuring on a weekly (or at least monthly) basis to ensure your initiative is operating from a position of health. These are the things that drive the "economic engine" (i.e. the growth, the health, the vitality) of your organization or initiative.

Brand Promise or Tagline — This component is far more optional than any other component of a strategic initiative plan. It is a short, memorable phrase that captures what your organization is all about. It can be your brand promise, such as what your customers or key stakeholders expect from you. It can be a marketing slogan, which is what you want to be remembered for. Or it can be a brief reference to the culture you want to exist. The key here is that it is short, memorable, and impactful.

To help a community begin to identify areas of entrepreneurial and innovation strength, the Venture Ecosystem Canvas can be used to take an assessment of existing resources, link and leverage positive assets, and formulate new initiatives to increase entrepreneurship. Once the initiatives are identified, the Strategic Initiative Planning Process can help organizations to streamline their efforts, become crystal clear on their role in the ecosystem, and determine a path forward to success.

PART 5:

Looking Ahead

CHAPTER 14:

Rise of the Best

What is the real talent, cost of living, and valuation arbitrage opportunity in the flyover states?

The impact of products and industries that didn't exist just five or ten years ago is a good measure of how entrepreneurship has become interwoven in our lives. There are seemingly infinite possibilities for innovation and, more significantly, an emergence of thriving entrepreneurial ecosystems throughout the country to support startup development. A talented workforce, affordable housing, and an agreeable cost of living can increasingly be found from Alabama to Wyoming. This allows entrepreneurs the opportunity to seek and find communities whose values and resources align with their needs.

A 2018 CNBC scorecard[242] ranked top states for businesses based on ten different categories and found flyover states to be well-represented. Utah was ranked third overall and Colorado and Minnesota closely followed at the 5th and 6th top states.

Among all categories, the scorecard identified the top three categories for business competitiveness as workforce, infrastructure, and cost of doing business. The top four states for the cost of doing business were Arkansas, Nebraska, Nevada, and Idaho (Missouri and Kentucky also were in the top ten). Indiana, Ohio, Minnesota, Kentucky, Nevada, and Utah were top states for infrastructure (defined as access to multiple modes and routes of transportation), and Colorado and Michigan were in the top ten states for availability and quality of workforce.

Flyover states also were frequently identified in other categories. The top three states for best cost of living were Mississippi, Arkansas, and Oklahoma; Michigan, Missouri, and Kansas were also in the top ten. Utah and Idaho were among the top five states noted for their solid, diverse economy, and Nebraska and Minnesota were in the top five states recognized for their high standards for education. Michigan and Minnesota were 3rd and 5th states, respectively, for innovation and technology.

Recognition with high rankings in these and other areas call deserved attention to flyover and other heartland states that have begun to distinguish themselves as entrepreneurial destinations. The proliferation and focal variety of ecosystems creates opportunities for entrepreneurs and their communities and also serves as a draw for other businesses, small and large.

Although these communities remain distant cousins to their California, New York, D.C., and Boston counterparts, change is coming. Some people may never give up their coastal proximity, but as young entrepreneurs grow into entrepreneurs with partners and children, the appeal of having their dollar go farther becomes more of a motivation. Continued growth and support of entrepreneurial talent will change flyover cities to destinations and new homes. As a critical mass of top talent gravitates to these and other large cities, they will become beacons for others. This, in turn, draws high tech companies, and the circle continues.

What is still mostly missing?

Even with traction at the ground floor of ecosystem building, for lasting sustainable change, small businesses need to have governmental policies that help them grow and not create additional barriers. The impact of insufficient entrepreneurial policy became blindingly clear throughout the COVID-19 crisis, as millions of small business owners were at risk of shutting down permanently due to diminished revenue and customers.[243] Advocacy groups like the Small Business Majority and the Kauffman Foundation's Start Us Up initiative recommend fundamental changes in current policies relating to the four pillars of ecosystem building.[244] Access to capital in a sufficient and timely manner proved to tip the scales on many small businesses' solvency. Not being aware of governmental emergency loan funds or not having accounts at local banks were some of the obstacles entrepreneurs faced with the Paycheck Protection Program of 2020.[245] With 83% of founders launching businesses without venture support or bank loans, it is imperative to provide roads to capital so entrepreneurs can access it when they need it most.[246]

Policy changes can also aid in mitigating risk for entrepreneurial talent. Concerns about student loan repayment, retirement and health insurance costs, and immigration visa red tape are just some of the issues that prevent brilliant entrepreneurial minds from taking a leap and starting a company.[247] The Kauffman Foundation's America's New Business Plan reports that 79% of new business owners do not feel supported by their government, and 60% of entrepreneurs feel like their government doesn't care about them at all.[248] For a truly innovative culture and robust community engagement, entrepreneurial talent must feel like their ideas and ventures are supported by leaders at all levels.

There are some easy ways to engage policy makers that the Startup Junkie and Conductor teams have utilized for maximum government engagement. Actions include administering a COVID-19 Impact Survey and sending the results to the office of the Governor; joining a Chamber of Commerce Government Relations team and advocating for entrepreneurs at Capitol Hill; inviting field staff of state senators to attend events and programs; highlight the stories of local entrepreneurs' successes and challenges; and hosting roundtable discussions with state congressman and other entrepreneurial support organizations. The ways to engage with policymakers are endless.But policymakers are only able to help if they know the issues, and it is the role of the ecosystem builder to help keep them informed. Policies and regulations must change for heartland ecosystems to thrive, and focusing on issues in the four pillar areas is the best place to start.

What is the outlook for the Rise of the Best?

The experience the Startup Junkie and Conductor teams have had in building lasting, viable venture ecosystems in unlikely places like Arkansas has shown that any region with the grit, tenacity, and determined ecosystem builders can do the same. The four pillars -- talent, culture, community engagement, and capital -- provide the template. The going is not easy. This is a long-term play that might take 20 years to really have a lasting impact. But the long march is worth it. To realize the "Rise of the Best" requires an understanding that the statistics show building entrepreneurial ecosystems are the "moneyball" economic development play to ensure greater job creation and sustained economic vitality. This movement must be led by entrepreneurs but must include ecosystem builders, investors, mentors, large enterprises, and public institutions to be really successful. The Chinese proverb says, 'The best time to plant a tree was 20 years ago, and the second best time is now." So what are you waiting for? The "Rise of the Best" can occur anywhere, even in your backyard, in that unexpected place that gets flown over every day.

Now, get to work!

Take the
Next Steps ...

There is no special training required to be a Startup Junkie. One only needs a passion for entrepreneurs, an innovative mindset, and a collaborative spirit. When these characteristics are paired with the four pillars of venture ecosystems - talent, culture, community engagement, and capital - startups are born and small businesses thrive. Chances are you're already doing this important work in your community, and have not yet considered your contribution to the ecosystem.

You may be a Startup Junkie if you are:

» An entrepreneur who wants to create the next best product of service

» An economic developer who wants to attract innovative industry

» A chamber executive who wants to increase small business engagement

» A government official who wants to strengthen local access to capital

» An educational leader who wants to retain talented graduates

» A civic champion who wants to cultivate a collaborative community

- » An angel investor who wants to grow early stage companies
- » A researcher who wants to commercialize scientific discoveries
- » A nonprofit director who wants to develop new strategies for continuous improvement

Startup Junkies can be from any sector, but are linked by a shared drive to empower entrepreneurs.

As you begin building your local ecosystem, please know the Startup Junkie and Conductor teams are here to help. Whether it's a walk through the Venture Ecosystem Building Canvas, guidance through the Strategic Initiative Planning Template, or providing one of our other proven tools for success, we want to help strengthen your work as you grow more startups and foster a more innovative environment. We know when entrepreneurs are supported, economies grow and communities thrive.

For a complimentary 30 minute strategy session with a member of the Startup Junkie or Conductor Team, please email us at *create@startupjunkieconsulting.com*. We'd be honored to help you and your team build a sustainable venture ecosystem in your own unexpected place.

Appendix/
Tools

Venture Ecosystem Building Canvas

Talent	Culture	Capital	Community Engagement
Who are the local innovators, inventors, or entrepreneurs who have built successful products, services, or companies?	What kinds of innovative social networks already exist that could be leveraged and what is the cadence of existing events, workshops, and programs?	What financial resources are available to fund the initiative?	What industries and competencies is the community most known for?
Who champions innovation and entrepreneurship in K-12?	What small businesses have generations of influence in the community?	What capital is available to invest in new ventures (angels, angel funds, VCs)?	What flagship enterprises exist within these industries?
What support organizations exist for the purpose of helping entrepreneurs?	What amenities is the community well known for that contributes to the culture and attracts and retains talent?	What's the level of angel or early-stage "Investor Acumen" among the community?	What needs do the flagship enterprises have that small businesses, entrepreneurs, or new initiatives can serve?
What colleges or universities exist within or in close proximity to our community?	How is the community plugged into global innovation and entrepreneurial initiatives?	What lending programs are available for non-traditional borrowers (e.g. low credit, criminal history)?	Who are the Entrepreneurial Leaders, Business Leaders, and Municipal Leaders in the community with the reputation, commitment, experience & resources to lead a new initiative?
What coding, data science, or STEM programs exist in close proximity to our community?	What role are successful entrepreneurs playing in mentoring and investing in startups?	Is there any SBIR/STTR support available?	Which organizations are willing to come together to serve as organizational champions for a new initiative?
What non-traditional workforce training is available?	What successful existing community initiatives have been launched within the past two years?	What other types of desirable capital is available (e.g. social, natural, built, etc.)?	What space is available for events/training, co-working, scale-up, or other programming?
What public, private, governmental research or innovation labs are in close proximity to our community that we could potentially leverage?	What is the leading cause of community initiatives to succeed?	How have new initiatives been funded in the past?	What resources are available out of town that entrepreneurs travel to obtain and how can those be replicated?
What's the level of maturity of the entrepreneurship and commercialization programs at the local university or college as evidenced by student and faculty spin-outs, licensed IP, and public and private funds raised?	How receptive and welcoming is the community to new ideas?	What technical assistance programs are available to assist financial management?	What is the view towards risk taking in the broader community?
How is the business acumen of those in the arts and culture being strengthened to increase the creative economy?	How diverse is the community in terms of demographics, beliefs, and experiences?	Who is helping entrepreneurs become investment ready?	Are there any "pockets" of expertise that could be leveraged?
When ventures successfully existed in the past what was the economic impact and	What "loosely organized" or organic activities are going on?	What financial institution is the most knowledgeable in SBA backed loans?	What is the "Leadership Climate" among the various leadership groups in the community (City Leaders, Chamber, Leaders, Economic

Identify Top Asset	Identify Supporting Strength
What emerged as the top asset in each of the four pillars?	Which supporting areas of strength emerged in each of the four pillars?
Talent:	Talent:
Culture:	Culture:
Capital:	Capital:
Community Engagement:	Community Engagement:
Initiative Quick Win	**Initiative Lasting Impact**
How can the top assets and supporting strengths be combined on an initiative that will bring a quick win for entrepreneurs/community?	How can the top assets and supporting strengths be combined on an initiative that will make a lasting impact for entrepreneurs/community?
Storytelling	
Who are the leaders in traditional media?	
Who are the social media influences?	
How does the community receive information?	
Who is interested in learning about new initiatives?	
What is the best way to engage with media players?	
How are community stories told?	

Strategic Initiative Planning Template

STRATEGIC INITIATIVE PLANNING (Name of Initiative)				
Mission/Purpose Statement	Why do we exist?			
Vision Statement	Where are we going over the next 3-5 years? What do we want to accomplish, be known for, etc.			
Values & Core Beliefs	*What do*	*we believe*	*and*	*value?*
Long Term Targets	*Three to five*	*year goals*	*to fulfill*	*the*	*vision*
Short Term Goals	*12-month*	*goals*	*we*	*must*	*accomplish*
KPIs	*Weekly*	*or monthly*	*indicators*	*of our*	*progress*
Brand Promise/Tagline	A simple phrase or statement that captures the essence of what we are doing - a rallying cry or slogan			

Author Bios

Jeff Amerine, M.S., PMP

Jeff is a nationally recognized leader in the creation of lasting venture ecosystems in unexpected places. Jeff has held senior leadership positions in nine startups and three Fortune 500 companies, and has made more than 90 early-stage investments into new ventures and small businesses, either directly or through the funds he manages. Jeff now leads Startup Junkie Consulting, and co-leads Innovation Junkie and Cadron Capital Partners. Previously Jeff served as Associate Vice Provost, Research and Economic Development, and Director of Technology Ventures at the University of Arkansas. In addition, Jeff is an adjunct professor and teaches entrepreneurship at the Sam M. Walton College of Business at the University of Arkansas. Early in his professional career, Jeff served six years as a United States Air Force officer, working in the Strategic Air Command as a missile launch officer and later in research and development acquisition. Jeff graduated from United States Naval Academy in 1984, holds a Master of Science in Operations Management from the University of Arkansas, and is a certified Project Management Professional (PMP).

Jeff D. Standridge, Ed.D.

Dr. Standridge helps organizations and their leaders generate sustained results in the areas of strategy, innovation, profit growth, organizational effectiveness, and leadership. Formerly a senior executive with Acxiom Corporation, he has led established and startup companies in North & South America, Europe, Asia, and the Middle East. Jeff serves as a Managing Director for the Conductor (*www.ARConductor.org*), is Cofounder of Cadron Capital Partners (*www.CadronCapital.com*), and teaches in the College of Business at the University of Central Arkansas (*www.UCA.edu*). Dr. Standridge has been an invited speaker, trainer, and consultant for numerous companies, institutions, and organizations across five continents. He is also the author of two best-selling books, *The Innovator's Field Guide: Accelerators for Entrepreneurs, Innovators, & Change Agents*, and *The Top Performer's Field Guide: Catalysts for Leaders, Superstars, and All Who Aspire to Be*. In addition to his executive coaching and customer-tailored consulting, he has received many accolades for his world class presentations, training programs, innovation sprints, and workshops.

Contributor Bios

Tiffany Henry, M.S.

Tiffany serves as the Director of Entrepreneurial Communities for the Conductor. In her role, she facilitates entrepreneurial and community programming in 11 counties in Central Arkansas. With a focus on rural and underserved regions, Tiffany supports sustainable ecosystem growth by providing individualized small business support and creating strategic partnerships with local economic development organizations. Tiffany holds a Master of Science in Psychology from Arkansas Tech University.

Grace Rains, M.B.A.

Grace serves as the Director of Operations at the Conductor. In her role, Grace guides the strategy and execution of Conductor & UCA Makerspace programming, runs the day to day operations of the Conductor, and collaborates closely with entrepreneurs and stakeholders to cultivate an inclusive entrepreneurial ecosystem. Grace has a background in healthcare, business development, and marketing, and she holds a Masters in Business Administration from the University of Central Arkansas.

Taylor Hasley

As the Executive Director at Startup Junkie Foundation, Taylor helps entrepreneurs quantify their ideas and develop a roadmap for achieving success. He is also responsible for directing the Fuel Accelerator program, which matches artificial intelligence startups from all over the world with regional enterprise partners to accelerate the development of tangible technology solutions, create jobs, and spur private investment. Prior to joining Startup Junkie, Taylor worked as a Senior Analyst at Zweig Group where he was primarily responsible for supporting the financials of Mergers & Acquisitions and Strategic Planning engagements. Taylor has also worked as an Analyst for NewRoad Capital Partners where he became well versed in all aspects of private equity. He graduated from the Sam M. Walton Honors College of Business in 2018 with a degree in Accounting and Finance, with a concentration in investments.

Morgan Scholz, M.A., SHRM-CP

Morgan is a business consultant with Startup Junkie Foundation. She supports entrepreneurs and innovators through consultation, resource referral, and community and educational programming. Her background is in development, human resources, and curriculum analysis, and she holds a Master of Arts in English Rhetoric, Composition, and Literacy from the University of Arkansas.

Caleb Talley

Caleb is the Director of Marketing, Events, and Community facing programs for the Startup Junkie Foundation. Caleb graduated from the University of Arkansas in 2015 with a bachelor's degree in journalism and political science. He cut his teeth as a reporter, photographer, and the opinion editor of the Times-Herald in Forrest City, Arkansas. During his time with the Times-Herald, he received national recognition for his work, including multiple Associated Press Managing Editors Awards for best hard news reporting and best news photography. He joined the Startup Junkie team after a two-year stint at Vowell, Inc., where he served as editor of *AY Magazine*, Arkansas' largest monthly lifestyle publication, and *Arkansas Money & Politics*, which he helped launch from a website to the largest monthly business and political magazine in the state.

Matthew Ward

Matthew is an Associate Consultant at Startup Junkie Foundation. He creates value for the entrepreneurial ecosystem by providing clarity to entrepreneurs and innovators, improving internal data processes, and supporting various impact programs. His background is in accounting, finance, and information systems, and he will complete his MBA from the University of Arkansas in Spring 2021.

Andrea M. Pampaloni, Ph.D.

An academic turned Communication Consultant, Andrea provides research, writing and marketing-communications services for corporate and nonprofit clients. Her expertise is in issues relevant to organizations and leaders, such as organizational relationship-building, culture, conflict, and superior-subordinate communication, and her goal always is to engage the audience. She enjoys collaborating with clients to understand their needs and to provide them with clear, accurate and comprehensive content through articles, blogs, white papers, social media plans or whatever traditional or unique product meets their unique needs.

Notes

1   https://higherlogicdownload.s3.amazonaws.com/NMSC/390e0055-2395-4d3b-af60-81b53974430d/UploadedImages/State_of_Main/A_Proven_Economic_Development_Strategy.pdf

2   https://www.entrepreneur.com/article/283616

3   https://www.entrepreneur.com/article/283616

4   https://www.forbes.com/places/united-states/

5   https://content.benetrends.com/blog/american-minority-business-ownership-a-look-at-the-stats#:~:text=Data%20Show%20Rise%20in%20Minority%20Ownership&text=Here%20are%20some%20additional%20statistics,%24237.5%20billion%20to%20%24254%20billion.

6   https://higherlogicdownload.s3.amazonaws.com/NMSC/390e0055-2395-4d3b-af60-81b53974430d/UploadedImages/State_of_Main/The_Importance_of_Inclusive_Entrepreneurship_Ecosystems.pdf

7   https://www.sba.gov/sites/default/files/advocacy/2018-Small-Business-Profiles-US.pdf

8   https://www.sciencedaily.com/releases/2018/01/180124113951.htm

9   https://www.wipo.int/pressroom/en/articles/2018/article_0005.html

10   https://www.forbes.com/places/united-states/

11   https://advocacy.sba.gov/2019/01/30/small-businesses-generate-44-percent-of-u-s-economic-activity/

12   https://www.sba.gov/sites/default/files/advocacy/2018-Small-Business-Profiles-US.pdf;   https://www.fundera.com/blog/small-business-employment-and-growth-statistics .

13   https://www.trade.gov/mas/ian/build/groups/public/@tg_ian/documents/webcontent/tg_ian_005538.pdf

14   thegedi.org/global-entrepreneurship-and-development-index/

15   https://www.inc.com/business-insider/25-best-countries-in-the-world-to-start-a-business.html

16   https://www.usnews.com/news/best-countries/entrepreneurship-rankings

17   https://www.fundera.com/blog/small-business-statistics

18   https://www.forbes.com/sites/williamdunkelberg/2018/08/06/small-business-powers-the-economy-forward/#1964ad7814ed

19   https://www.census.gov/newsroom/blogs/research-matters/2018/02/bfs.html

20   https://fitsmallbusiness.com/entrepreneurship-statistics/

21   https://www.fundera.com/blog/small-business-statistics

22   https://thegedi.org/global-entrepreneurship-and-development-index/

23   The GEI considers entrepreneurial abilities (the population's acceptance and support for entrepreneurs), personal abilities (motivated and educated entrepreneurs starting in tech-related sectors), and aspiration (introduction and growth of new prod-

ucts/services). The GEM combines several qualities into three sub-sections: factor-driven (develop and sell cheap products built by unskilled labor), efficiency-driven (uses more efficient process with better quality), and innovation-driven (new, improved products help expand service sector).

24   GEM

25   GEDI

26   https://business.financialpost.com/entrepreneur/1121-biz-rs-spence-jerusalem

27   https://jel.jewish-languages.org/words/119

28   http://www.startupchile.org/es/impact/

29   https://t-hub.co/about-us/

30   https://www.forbes.com/sites/knowledgewharton/2016/05/12/george-washington-americas-first-entrepreneur/#2e832c995a89

31   https://www.fi.edu/benjamin-franklin/inventions; http://www.benfranklin300.org/etc_article_entrepreneur.htm

32   http://www.benfranklin300.org/etc_article_entrepreneur.htm

33   http://www.ltbn.com/hall_of_fame/Edison.html

34   https://squareup.com/townsquare/the-history-of-american-entrepreneurship

35   https://www.britannica.com/biography/Madam-C-J-Walker

36   https://www.forbes.com/profile/sara-blakely/#218d45f676bb

37   https://en.wikipedia.org/wiki/Daymond_John

38   Stam, E., & Spigel, E. (2016). Entrepreneurial Ecosystems. *Utrecht School of Economics, Tjalling C. Koopmans Research Institute.*

39   https://www.kauffman.org/-/media/kauffman_org/research-reports-and-covers/2015/10/enabling_entrepreneurial_ecosystems.pdf

40   https://www.forbes.com/sites/danisenberg/2011/05/25/introducing-the-entrepreneurship-ecosystem-four-defining-characteristics/#6b4e127d5fe8; https://assets.aspeninstitute.org/content/uploads/files/content/docs/pubs/FINAL%20Ecosystem%20Toolkit%20Draft_print%20version.pdf; https://assets.aspeninstitute.org/content/uploads/files/content/docs/pubs/FINAL%20Ecosystem%20Toolkit%20Draft_print%20version.pdf

41   https://www.kauffman.org/entrepreneurial-ecosystem-building-playbook-draft-2/introduction#aletterfromvictorhwang

42   Meyers, Maria E., and Kate P. Hodel. *Beyond Collisions: How to Build your Entrepreneurial Infrastructure.* Wavesource LLC, 2017, p. 29.

43   https://www.kauffman.org/what-we-do/entrepreneurship

44   http://entrepreneurial-revolution.com/who-we-are/

45   https://www.eonetwork.org/why-join/the-eo-experience/

46   https://www.genglobal.org/about-gen

47   https://www.tugboatinstitute.com/what-is-evergreen/

48   https://tech.co/news/ecosystem-builders-startup-growth-2018-05

49   https://www.mainstreet.org/ourwork/projectspotlight/entrepreneurialecosystems

50   https://inbia.org/

51   https://medium.com/make-innovation-work/the-beneficiaries-of-corporate-entrepreneurship-programs-61dc41ab2740

52   http://www.catecosta.com/wp-content/uploads/2017/07/White-Paper-_-Re-Examining-Entrepreneurship-Support-Structures-to-Improve-Outcomes-for-Under-Served-Entrepreneurs-_-Venture-Catalyst-Consulting.pdf

53   https://www.wired.com/insights/2014/02/university-ideal-startup-platform/

54   https://www.entrepreneur.com/article/294798; https://www.techrepublic.com/article/accelerators-vs-incubators-what-startups-need-to-know/; https://microventures.com/accelerators-vs-incubators

55   https://www.entrepreneur.com/article/294798; https://www.techrepublic.com/article/accelerators-vs-incubators-what-startups-need-to-know/; https://microventures.com/accelerators-vs-incubators

56   https://hbr.org/2014/05/what-an-entrepreneurial-ecosystem-actually-is; https://microventures.com/accelerators-vs-incubators

57   https://www.dreamit.com/#meaningful-experience

58   https://costarters.co/impact/

59   https://www.idealab.com/

60   https://startupnation.com/

61   https://www.idealab.com/

62   https://www.blackgirlventures.org/

63   https://ruralinnovation.us/our-work/; https://www.corifund.com/

64   https://forwardcities.org/

65   https://yec.co/

66   https://www.startupjunkie.org/our-team

67   www.arconductor.org/about

68   https://championtraveler.com/news/flyover-states-flight-data-shows-which-states-americans-think-are-boring/

69   https://www.usatoday.com/story/travel/flights/2017/11/15/flyover-states/860668001/; https://www.britannica.com/place/Middle-West

70   https://www.bestplaces.net/economy/state/nebraska

71   https://www.census.gov/newsroom/press-releases/2018/estimates-national-state.html

72   https://www.entrepreneur.com/article/307177

73   https://www.washingtonpost.com/news/innovations/wp/2014/09/22/why-innovation-and-start-ups-are-thriving-in-flyover-country/?utm_term=.3b454fee0443

74   https://observer.com/2019/01/flyover-tech-jp-morgan-healthcare-investment-conference/; https://www.washingtonpost.com/news/innovations/wp/2014/09/22/why-innovation-and-start-ups-are-thriving-in-flyover-country/?utm_term=.c436b7b63bb0; https://www.inc.com/anna-hensel/omaha-startups-experiencing-second-wave-of-growth.html

75   https://venturebeat.com/2016/10/22/3-things-the-flyover-states-need-to-compete-with-silicon-valley/; https://www.washingtonpost.com/news/innovations/wp/2014/09/22/why-innovation-and-start-ups-are-thriving-in-flyover-country/?utm_term=.3b454fee0443

76   https://venturebeat.com/2016/10/22/3-things-the-flyover-states-need-to-compete-with-silicon-valley/

77   https://livability.com/best-places/best-cities-for-entrepreneurs/2016

78   https://livability.com/ne/omaha/real-estate/why-omaha-may-be-the-best-place-to-live-and-work-in-the-midwest

79   https://livability.com/ne/omaha/real-estate/why-omaha-may-be-the-best-place-to-live-and-work-in-the-midwest; https://www.inc.com/anna-hensel/omaha-startups-experiencing-second-wave-of-growth.html

80   https://fundingsage.com/entrepreneurial-ecosystem-spotlight-tulsa-ok/

81   https://www.business.org/business/startup/top-cities-for-entrepreneurs-and-startups/

82   https://techcrunch.com/2017/08/02/here-are-the-best-startup-cities-in-the-midwest/

83   https://venturebeat.com/2018/06/09/a-guide-to-minnesotas-startup-community/

84   https://venturebeat.com/2018/06/09/a-guide-to-minnesotas-startup-community/

85   https://medium.com/disruptmidwest/how-are-twin-cities-mayors-supporting-the-startup-ecosystem-7c9b42c97b86

86   https://www.startupjunkie.org/

87   https://www.inc.com/magazine/202002/emily-canal/boise-idaho-tech-startup-hub-2019-surge-cities.html

88   https://www.inc.com/surge-cities

89   https://www.inc.com/magazine/202002/emily-canal/boise-idaho-tech-startup-hub-2019-surge-cities.html

90   https://www.idahowomen.org/

91   https://www.inc.com/magazine/202002/cameron-albert-deitch/superfast-internet-broadband-gigabit-chattanooga-smaller-city.html

92   https://www.chattanoogachamber.com/incubator

93   https://www.epicentermemphis.org/

94   http://neverstop.co/

95   http://the800.org/index.html

96   https://www.kauffman.org/kauffman-index/reporting/~/media/9f685e8c214248f0884fa21416f6b03e.ashx

97   https://www.inc.com/paul-spiegelman/3-reasons-entrepreneurs-love-texas.html

98   https://www.cnbc.com/2018/06/27/top-10-states-that-are-winning-the-war-for-talent.html

99   https://www.dallasnews.com/business/business/2019/01/15/texas-no-1-usforfemale-entrepreneurs-new-study

100   https://www.crowdspring.com/blog/startups-entrepreneurs-best-startup-cities-us/

101   http://worldpopulationreview.com/states/texas-population/

102   https://www.cnbc.com/2018/06/27/top-10-states-that-are-winning-the-war-for-talent.html

103   http://www.dailycamera.com/boulder-business/ci_32122446/report-seeks-ingredients-boulders-economic-secret-sauce

104   https://www.nerdwallet.com/blog/utilities/best-metro-areas-for-young-entrepreneurs-2017/

105   https://fundingsage.com/entrepreneurial-ecosystem-spotlight-ann-arbor-mi/

106   https://www.cnbc.com/2018/06/27/top-10-states-that-are-winning-the-war-for-talent.html

107   https://entrypointmi.com/2018/10/30/2018-detroit-report/

108   https://www.shrm.org/hr-today/trends-and-forecasting/special-reports-and-expert-views/pages/impact-hiring_a_double_bottom-line_solution.aspx

109   https://onlinelibrary.wiley.com/doi/full/10.1111/gec3.12359

110   https://www.smecc.org/frederick_terman.htm

111   https://www.pbs.org/transistor/album1/addlbios/terman.html

112   http://cmovc.com/5-key-factors-in-creating-an-active-startup-ecoystem-flywheel/

113   https://mcmillonstudio.uark.edu/

114   https://www.arconductor.org/makerspace

115   https://gabbybows.com/

116   https://wisepocketproducts.com/

117   https://theconversation.com/help-your-children-play-out-a-story-and-watch-them-become-more-creative-61194

118   https://www.fastcompany.com/3023094/science-says-art-will-make-your-kids-better-thinkers-and-nicer-people

119   https://www.inc.com/tom-foster/how-kids-become-entrepreneurs.html

120   https://www.thebalancecareers.com/what-is-talent-management-really-1919221

121   http://www.futureofbusinessandtech.com/education-and-careers/developing-talent-drives-engagement-and-business-success

122   https://www.inc.com/alison-eyring/4-ways-fast-growing-companies-develop-talent-for-free.html;   https://www.forbes.com/sites/steveolenski/2015/07/20/8-key-tactics-for-developing-employees/#72eb1286373d

123   https://www.entrepreneur.com/article/280134

124   https://www.entrepreneur.com/article/299088;   https://www.inc.com/young-entrepreneur-council/why-professional-networking-is-missing-piece-to-your-success.html

125   https://www.oecd.org/cfe/leed/21561596.pdf; https://www.networkkansas.com/blog/ntks-blog/2013/04/08/7-traits-of-entrepreneurial-communities

126   https://gothamculture.com/what-is-organizational-culture-definition/; http://www.businessdictionary.com/definition/organizational-culture.html

127   https://www.investopedia.com/articles/personal-finance/101014/10-characteristics-successful-entrepreneurs.asp;   https://www.inc.com/sujan-patel/10-essential-characteristics-of-highly-successful-.html

128   https://www.business.com/articles/12-ways-foster-entrepreneurial-culture/

129   https://medium.com/@socialtrendspot/4-elements-of-entrepreneurial-culture-and-how-to-incorporate-them-into-the-social-sector-b4baee7e3be1; https://www.fastcompany.com/90158100/how-to-build-an-entrepreneurial-culture-5-tips-from-eric-ries

130   https://www.fastcompany.com/90158100/how-to-build-an-entrepreneurial-culture-5-tips-from-eric-ries; https://www.business.com/articles/12-ways-foster-entrepreneurial-culture/

131   https://www.business.com/articles/12-ways-foster-entrepreneurial-culture/;   https://medium.com/@socialtrendspot/4-elements-of-entrepreneurial-culture-and-how-to-incorporate-them-into-the-social-sector-b4baee7e3be1; https://www.entrepreneur.com/article/293677

132   https://www.entrepreneur.com/article/349419;   https://hbr.org/2013/12/how-diversity-can-drive-innovation

133   https://www.explorevr.org/sites/explorevr.org/files/files/What%20is%20Business%20Engagement.pdf

134   https://aese.psu.edu/research/centers/cecd/engagement-toolbox/engagement/what-is-community-engagement

135   https://www.allbusiness.com/the-benefits-of-community-engagement-for-your-business-16768-1.html

136   https://aese.psu.edu/research/centers/cecd/engagement-toolbox/engagement/what-is-community-engagement

137   http://www.startupchampions.co/#benefits

138   https://www.kauffman.org/eship-summit/playbook/

139   https://sites.google.com/view/eshipcommunitydashboard/

140   https://groundworkusa.org/wp-content/uploads/2018/03/GWUSA_Best-Practices-for-Meaningful-Community-Engagement-Tip-Sheet.pdf; https://www.communityplanningtoolkit.org/sites/default/files/Engagement.pdf

141   https://www.forbes.com/sites/victorhwang/2013/10/31/growing-a-venture-capital-ecosystem/#2428c0c1a11b
142   https://www.citylab.com/life/2018/03/the-extreme-geographic-inequality-of-high-tech-venture-capital/552026/
143   https://smallbusiness.chron.com/importance-funding-business-59.html; https://startupnation.com/start-your-business/seed-money-entrepreneurs-get/
144   https://www.entrepreneur.com/article/287001;https://www.entrepreneur.com/article/80024
145
146   https://startupnation.com/start-your-business/seed-money-entrepreneurs-get/
147   http://www.ecosysteminsights.org/entrepreneurial-experience-supports-the-best-vcs-from-other-investors/
148   https://www.forbes.com/sites/victorhwang/2013/10/31/growing-a-venture-capital-ecosystem/#2428c0c1a11b
149   https://www.forbes.com/sites/alejandrocremades/2018/09/25/how-angel-investors-and-angel-groups-work/#39fbda7476dc
150   https://www.thebalancesmb.com/what-are-angel-investors-392985
151   https://startupnation.com/start-your-business/seed-money-entrepreneurs-get/
152   https://smallbiztrends.com/2008/11/the-size-of-angel-investments.html;   https://www.forbes.com/sites/allbusiness/2015/02/05/20-things-all-entrepreneurs-should-know-about-angel-investors/#1b721134c1aa;   https://www.thebalancesmb.com/angel-investor-2947066
153   https://www.thebalancesmb.com/angel-investor-2947066
154   https://www.thebalancesmb.com/the-7-things-angel-investors-are-looking-for-2948104
155   https://www.thebalancesmb.com/what-are-angel-investors-392985
156   https://www.thebalancesmb.com/the-7-things-angel-investors-are-looking-for-2948104
157   http://www.ecosysteminsights.org/how-do-angel-investors-rationalize-risk/
158   https://www.thebalancesmb.com/what-are-angel-investors-392985; https://www.hban.org/Syndicates/Syndicates.162.html
159   https://www.thebalancesmb.com/what-are-angel-investors-392985
160   http://pointsandfigures.com/2018/03/13/16-best-practices-for-angel-groups/
161   http://pointsandfigures.com/2018/03/13/16-best-practices-for-angel-groups/
162   https://www.angelcapitalassociation.org/data/Documents/Resources/AngelCapitalEducation/ACEF_BEST_PRACTICES_Due_Diligence.pdf
163   https://journals.sagepub.com/doi/abs/10.1177/0266242612453932
164   https://digitalcommons.pepperdine.edu/cgi/viewcontent.cgi?article=1009&context=jef;https://medium.com/ceoquest/funding-exits-chapter-3-the-investor-continuum-3585656afd9f
165   https://betakit.com/ask-an-investor-should-i-celebrate-my-funding-round/; http://www.businessworld.in/article/Here-s-Why-We-must-Stop-Celebrating-When-Startups-Get-Funded-by-VCs/04-04-2018-145384/
166   http://fundlibrary.com/features/columns/page.asp?id=14222
167   https://www.forbes.com/sites/alejandrocremades/2018/08/19/debt-vs-equity-financinpros-and-cons-for-entrepreneurs/#25f675f46900
168   https://www.upcounsel.com/non-dilutive

169   https://www.lawtrades.com/blog/answers/usual-share-percentage-seed-round/

170   https://www.inc.com/alex-baydin/how-to-build-a-scalable-tech-business-without-vc-funding.html; https://www.forbes.com/sites/martinzwilling/2016/08/31/smart-entrepreneurs-build-startups-without-investors/#7b40851d41ba

171   @£

172

173   http://www.ecosysteminsights.org/how-do-the-first-few-years-of-a-scaleups-life-differ-across-countries/

174   https://fyi.extension.wisc.edu/downtown-market-analysis/putting-your-research-to-work/entrepreneurship/

175   https://www.strongtowns.org/journal/2016/4/19/how-to-encourage-entrepreneurship-in-your-town

176   https://www.natcapsolutions.org/LASER/LASER_Building-Entrepreneurial-Communities.pdf

177   https://www.americaninno.com/minne/why-minnesota-is-a-hub-for-food-and-agriculture-innovation/

178   https://www.google.com/search?q=washington+dc+biotech+entrepreneurs&rlz=1C1CHFX_enUS757US757&oq=washington+dc+biotech+entrepreneurs&aqs=chrome..69i57.9551j0j7&sourceid=chrome&ie=UTF-8

179   https://www.nwahomepage.com/knwa/startups-across-the-country-coming-to-northwest-arkansas-to-work-with-big-companies/

180   https://www.forbes.com/sites/petercohan/2017/07/21/dont-try-to-make-your-city-the-next-silicon-valley/#3e8e9b971d3d

181   https://www.inc.com/steve-blank/vc-steve-blank-your-established-company-can-innovate-just-as-fast-as-a-startup-heres-how.html

182   https://www.inc.com/inc5000/index.html

183   https://startupwi.org/events

184   https://www.1millioncups.com/about

185   https://wedc.org/programs/?fwp_programsresources_category=program-entrepreneurs%2Cprogram-wedc-program

186   https://wisconsintechnologycouncil.com/about/

187   https://bus.wisc.edu/centers/weinert/events

188   https://www.forbes.com/sites/groupthink/2018/02/18/businesses-move-to-the-midwest-first-stop-columbus/#1d1914173721

189   https://columbus.startupweek.co/

190   https://fisher.osu.edu/news/boss-competition-brings-out-very-best-student-ideas

191   https://fundingsage.com/entrepreneurial-ecosystem-spotlight-columbus-oh/

192   https://ventureohio.org/our-plan/

193   https://www.kcchamber.com/what-we-do/big-5-initiatives/entrepreneurship

194   https://www.gobankingrates.com/making-money/entrepreneur/state-with-best-cities-for-entrepreneurs/

195   https://fundingsage.com/entrepreneurial-ecosystem-spotlight-kansas-city-mo/

196   https://www.kcsourcelink.com/

197   https://www.missouritechnology.com/innovation-centers

198   https://www.kauffman.org/-/media/kauffman_org/research-reports-and-covers/2014/09/examining_the_connections_within_the_startup_ecosystem.pdf

199   https://www.inc.com/steve-blank/vc-steve-blank-your-established-company-can-innovate-just-as-fast-as-a-startup-heres-how.html

200   https://innov8rs.co/news/finally-move-innovation-theatre-innovation-competency/

201   https://medium.com/the-moment-is/3-signals-of-innovation-theatre-to-watch-out-for-8c2e29d4dcf3

202   https://www.inc.com/steve-blank/vc-steve-blank-your-established-company-can-innovate-just-as-fast-as-a-startup-heres-how.html

203   https://innov8rs.co/news/finally-move-innovation-theatre-innovation-competency/

204   Utrecht

205   https://www.entrepreneur.com/article/280134

206   https://deepblue.lib.umich.edu/bitstream/handle/2027.42/139028/1376_Sanchez-Burks.pdf?sequence=1&isAllowed=y

207   https://www.kauffman.org/-/media/kauffman_org/research-reports-and-covers/2014/09/examining_the_connections_within_the_startup_ecosystem.pdf

208   https://deepblue.lib.umich.edu/bitstream/handle/2027.42/139028/1376_Sanchez-Burks.pdf?sequence=1&isAllowed=y

209   https://www.sba.gov/about-sba

210   https://www.entrepreneur.com/article/318024

211   https://www.sciencedirect.com/science/article/abs/pii/S0001879105000680?via%3Dihub

212   https://the-jade.org/mentors-giving-entrepreneurs-an-unfair-advantage/

213   https://techcrunch.com/2015/03/22/mentors-are-the-secret-weapons-of-successful-startups/

214   https://www.forbes.com/sites/kateharrison/2018/10/30/new-study-reveals-entrepreneurs-need-more-mentoring/#754cc6df7819

215   https://we.st/innovation-tools/mentorship/building-mentorship-program-matching-mentors-mentees/;   https://www.sciencedirect.com/science/article/abs/pii/S0001879105000680?via%3Dihub

216   https://www.youtube.com/watch?v=PaXO9Uab6K0

217   https://deepblue.lib.umich.edu/bitstream/handle/2027.42/139028/1376_Sanchez-Burks.pdf?sequence=1&isAllowed=y

218   https://deepblue.lib.umich.edu/bitstream/handle/2027.42/139028/1376_Sanchez-Burks.pdf?sequence=1&isAllowed=y

219   https://www.mowgli.org.uk/what-we-do/our-programs/entrepreneur-mentoring-program

220   https://medium.com/west-stringfellow/entrepreneurial-mentorship-and-its-competitive-advantage-62d83146b268

221   https://medium.com/swlh/whats-the-difference-between-a-mentor-an-advisor-and-a-coach-b72165bba983

222   https://www.kent.edu/yourtrainingpartner/know-difference-between-coaching-and-mentoring

223   https://www.forbes.com/sites/ellevate/2015/10/15/the-difference-between-a-coach-and-a-mentor/#6da23b407556;   https://www.kent.edu/yourtrainingpartner/know-difference-between-coaching-and-mentoring

224   https://odk.org/odk-careers/mentoring-center/ten-tips-for-mentees/reasonable-expectations-for-mentoring/

225   https://www.forbes.com/sites/robertamatuson/2018/11/14/how-to-be-a-great-mentee-and-mentor/#56335fb3f882

226   https://deepblue.lib.umich.edu/bitstream/handle/2027.42/139028/1376_ Sanchez-Burks.pdf?sequence=1&isAllowed=y

227   https://www.entrepreneur.com/encyclopedia/networking

228   https://www.entrepreneur.com/encyclopedia/networking; https://www. startupgrind.com/blog/6-ways-to-improve-your-entrepreneur-network-2/; https://www. success.com/8-proven-networking-strategies-of-successful-entrepreneurs/; https://www. forbes.com/sites/susanrittscher/2012/05/31/six-keys-to-successful-networking-for-en-trepreneurs/#580aefa1580b; https://www.forbes.com/sites/theyec/2018/06/26/entre-preneurial-networking-10-approaches-you-can-use/#6a0ae8afe428

229   https://www.truesocialmetrics.com/blog/why-measuring-follow-ers-is-bad-idea?locale=en_US

230   https://www.pewinternet.org/2018/03/01/social-media-use-in-2018/

231   https://www.pewinternet.org/2018/03/01/social-media-use-in-2018/

232   https://www.searchenginejournal.com/seo-101/meet-search-engines/#close

233   https://blog.hubspot.com/marketing/best-times-post-pin-tweet-social-me-dia-infographic

234   https://www.convinceandconvert.com/social-media-strategy/7-surpris-ing-statistics-about-twitter-in-america/

235   https://sproutsocial.com/insights/new-social-media-demographics/

236   https://www.pewinternet.org/2018/03/01/social-media-use-in-2018/

237   https://medium.com/@HeathEvans/content-is-king-essay-by-bill-gates-1996-df74552f80d9

238   https://clearimpact.com/solutions/asset-based-community-development/

239   https://strategicdoing.net/intro/

240   https://www.startupjunkie.org/podcast

241   https://www.amazon.com/Strategic-Acceleration-Succeed-Speed-Life/ dp/1593155646/ref=tmm_pap_swatch_0?_encoding=UTF8&qid=&sr=

242   https://www.cnbc.com/2018/07/10/americas-top-states-for-business-2018. html

243   https://www.mainstreet.org/blogs/national-main-street-center/2020/04/14/ just-released-data-from-the-survey-on-the-impact-o?CommunityKey=c40a84d1-46b2-465c-985c-c08ed69081ab&tab=

244   https://smallbusinessmajority.org/our-research/roadmap-to-recov-ery; https://www.startusupnow.org/wp-content/uploads/sites/12/2020/04/Ameri-cas-New-Business-Plan-Rebuilding-Better.pdf

245   https://www.barrons.com/articles/smaller-banks-doled-out-bulk-of-ppp-loans-fed-data-show-51588677303

246   https://www.startusupnow.org/wp-content/uploads/sites/12/2020/04/ Americas-New-Business-Plan-Rebuilding-Better.pdf

247   https://www.startusupnow.org/wp-content/uploads/sites/12/2019/10/ Kauffman_AmericasNewBusinessPlanWhitepaper_October2019.pdf; https://small-businessmajority.org/our-research/roadmap-to-recovery

248   https://www.startusupnow.org/wp-content/uploads/sites/12/2019/10/ Kauffman_AmericasNewBusinessPlanWhitepaper_October2019.pdf

CPSIA information can be obtained
at www.ICGtesting.com
Printed in the USA
JSHW031204190121
10963JS00004B/17